PLANNING FOR
PLAY

Strategies for Guiding Preschool Learning

Kristen Kemple, PhD

Gryphon House
www.gryphonhouse.com

Copyright ©2017 Kristen Kemple

Published by Gryphon House, Inc.

P. O. Box 10, Lewisville, NC 27023
800.638.0928; 877.638.7576 (fax)
Visit us on the web at www.gryphonhouse.com.

Library of Congress Cataloging-in-Publication Data

The cataloging-in-publication data is registered with the Library of Congress for ISBN 978-0-87659-716-3.

Bulk Purchase

Gryphon House books are available for special premiums and sales promotions as well as for fund-raising use. Special editions or book excerpts also can be created to specifications. For details, call 800.638.0928.

Disclaimer

Gryphon House, Inc., cannot be held responsible for damage, mishap, or injury incurred during the use of or because of activities in this book. Appropriate and reasonable caution and adult supervision of children involved in activities and corresponding to the age and capability of each child involved are recommended at all times. Do not leave children unattended at any time. Observe safety and caution at all times.

■■

Dedication

This book is dedicated to my parents, Elizabeth and Roger, who allowed me the freedom of play, and to my children, Nick and Susi, who remind me daily of its power.

Table of Contents

Introduction

Play has begun to take a back seat in the lives of young children. This is a disturbing state of affairs, which seems to be happening for several reasons. With changes in technology and an increase in "screen time" in children's daily lives, they spend less time playing and more time in passive and sedentary activities. Increasing emphasis on high-stakes testing of narrowly defined skills has led to a belief that time spent in classrooms on play is not learning time and is, therefore, wasted time. Even in after-school programs and extracurricular activities, children spend less time in play and more time on structured activities. Educators and researchers in early childhood development are experiencing a sense of disbelief that they are having to defend the value of play for kindergarten and primary-aged children, let alone for those as young as preschoolers!

The forces that are pushing play out of the lives of young children are forces rooted in misunderstandings about the way young children develop and learn. Although play is not the only way children progress in the early years, it is an indispensable context and process for learning.

This book is designed to illustrate the value of both free play and guided play in preschool children's learning and development. In each chapter you will find anecdotes that explore the possible ways children play, what they can learn from their self-motivated engagement, and how teachers can support that learning. In other words, play is presented not as an activity that is simply allowed to happen but instead as a process that requires teachers to be knowledgeable, to plan well, and to be intentional. To make the most of preschoolers' play, teachers should consider important child-development and learning goals that can be supported through play, as well as specific strategies for capitalizing on and enhancing the power of play for children's educational benefit and well-being.

one | 1 |

Promoting Development and Learning

In Miss Abela's full-day preschool class, play is at the center of the program. Children engage in about an hour of indoor play and an hour of outdoor play in the morning and again in the afternoon. A visitor to the program will observe children engaged in free play as well as teacher-guided play. The other four hours of the day include meals and snacks, rest time, and teacher-led small and large group activities of about ten to twenty minutes each. In those group activities, children participate in music and art experiences; listen to and discuss storybooks and informational books; write and draw in journals; engage in science and math activities; and learn letter recognition through fun, engaging, and meaningful lessons.

During large and small group activities, Miss Abela uses diverse learning formats. She knows young children do not learn everything through play, and she uses a variety of developmentally appropriate teaching strategies that allow for active participation by the children. At the same time, she knows young children learn a great deal through play and need play for a variety of developmental reasons. Miss Abela plans thoughtfully and intentionally to maximize play-based learning and development. The children in her class are learning, growing, and thriving. They are enjoying their preschool experience.

As professionals committed to early childhood education, we want to see children reach their greatest potential and contribute to a bright and better future. A wealth of research-based practices is available to make these goals possible. In developmentally appropriate preschool programs, teachers promote children's learning and development in ways that are attentive to the needs, interests, abilities, and developmental capabilities of individual children. They do this in ways that are sensitive to the general age range of the group and to the social, cultural, and experiential backgrounds of the young children in their care. The teaching expertise involved in providing for and supporting play stands among the many crucial skills a preschool teacher will use as part of developmentally appropriate practice.

What do parents want for their young children? Virtually all want to see their children grow to be happy and successful adults. When choosing a preschool program, some parents may not see their decision as particularly important to their child's long-term outcomes. Among those who do see the importance of the decision, there may be many different ideas regarding what kind of preschool program will best contribute to putting their children on a path toward growing up as happy and successful people. Some believe a preschool program in which children spend a great deal of time in freely chosen exploration and play is the best choice. Many others believe the ideal is a highly structured environment in which teachers lead most activities, getting their child started as early as possible in acquiring basic academic skills. In these considerations, play and academic learning are frequently cast as two very different and unrelated things. But are they?

The distinction between a preschool program in which children engage in enjoyable play and a preschool program in which children engage in important learning is a false dichotomy. As we will see in the coming pages, children experience a great deal of important learning through the process of play. There is no need to choose between play and learning. In fact, choosing to eliminate or severely restrict play is in effect choosing to seriously restrict young children's learning.

> There is no need to choose between play and learning. In fact, choosing to eliminate or severely restrict play is in effect choosing to seriously restrict young children's learning.

When parents send their child to preschool, they are entrusting to the teacher their child's intellect and so much more. All of the various aspects of a child's self—social, emotional, cognitive, physical, and linguistic—come along to school. These domains are all interconnected; each part of the child influences the other parts. For example, a young child's social competence is connected to his ability to use language to communicate. His budding literacy is built upon his grasp of spoken language. A child who is preoccupied with fears and worries is limited in his ability to engage in activities and thinking that could further his cognitive growth. A child who is not well-nourished or who is sleep-deprived may feel too grouchy or lethargic to participate in play with peers. These are but a few examples of the complex network of connections that make up the whole child. To educate and care for a young child, it is important to recognize these multiple and mutual influences. We cannot nurture and teach a child's cognitive self in the absence of fully attending to the other parts of his being.

Play and Academic Growth

How does play contribute to academic growth? Give yourself a moment to consider this question. Some teachers may think first of obvious and seemingly direct methods for connecting play with academics. For example, these may include such practices as placing reading and writing materials in the dramatic play center and blocks center and suggesting ways that children may choose to use them in their play. Paper and pens can be used to create a grocery list. A book may be selected and placed in the block center to provide ideas about different kinds of buildings to construct or different heavy equipment to imagine using in the construction of those buildings. Lullaby song/picture books can be placed in the book corner, the housekeeping center, or by the bean-bag chair in the quiet area for the purpose of singing, reading, and rocking dolls to sleep. Providing inset puzzles that are comprised of the letters of the alphabet is another direct way that play opportunities can support academic activity, as is asking children to count the number of Legos they used to create a barnyard fence for a collection of plastic cows. Providing simple board games that require children to count out the number of spaces to move their game piece is another example. All of these are, indeed, very useful and age-appropriate practices for preschoolers.

If we look even more deeply, we see that play can also contribute in ways that are less obviously, though not less importantly, related to academics. For example, you might equip the dramatic play center with a rich array of interesting materials related

to a thematic unit under study. Imagine that your unit theme is entomologists. From a preschooler's perspective, this is a very big and exciting name for scientists who study insects. You equip the dramatic play center with plastic insects, jars and nets for catching and containing the insects, binoculars and magnifying glasses for spotting and closely examining the insects, clipboards for drawing the insects, and field guides for identification. After reading a book about entomologists and perhaps taking children on a playground bug hunt, some children may choose to create a play scenario in the dramatic play center about searching for insects in the jungle. Through constructing the implicit script of their play, they are learning about narrative, dialogue, plot, and character. Even though they likely don't yet have the names for these components, they have a basic awareness that helps them to better understand stories and to create their own. They learn new vocabulary as they play with materials and practice the new content and terminology they are hearing.

As children pretend, take on roles, and assign new meaning to objects—for example, pretending that a pair of tongs or a couple of fingers are tweezers—they exercise and further develop their abilities in symbolic thinking. They begin to understand, for example, that the mark that looks like the letter A means something, just as the mark that looks like the number *4* represents something different.

As children engage in play around this interesting theme, they negotiate the play, resolving such important questions as who will be who and what will happen. They encounter differences of opinion as the play unfolds, which call for compromise. With gentle support and guidance from their teacher, children are developing their social and emotional competence. Children's social and emotional competence is predictive of their success in school and life, and nurturing relationships are essential to optimal development (IOM and NRC, 2012; Shonkoff and Phillips, 2000).

As children engage in play in the insect-themed dramatic play corner, playing in their own ways and following their own ideas, they have the opportunity to have fun, rejuvenate, release, and relax from some of the more structured parts of their preschool program. In developmentally appropriate preschool programs, teachers are mindful of the importance of pacing and balance in the daily schedule, and they avoid a routine that lines up several teacher-led, sedentary activities in a row. When children experience playful breaks from more structured learning experiences, when they are given "breathing room," they experience less stress and are better able to return to more structured activities, such as listening to a book being read aloud, attentively observing a demonstration by the teacher, and other experiences that require sitting still and being attentive for a brief period of time during a teacher-directed activity.

Now let's look at a brief sampling of what research tells us about the contribution of play to some specific abilities and concepts in social-emotional, mathematical, and literacy learning, as well as growth in self-regulation and creativity. We will also look at examples of what these might look like in a typical preschool classroom such as your own.

The Social-Emotional Domain:
Establishing Friendly Peer Relationships

As children engage in play, they learn how to engage in social problem solving. The social problems that children encounter as they play include how to share limited resources, how to enter an in-progress play situation, how to negotiate who will play which role in a pretend situation, and what twists and turns the plot will take as they act out their ideas. These skills contribute to the quality and pleasure of children's friendships and their peer interactions.

OBSERVE AND LEARN:
Maurice and Sami Enjoy Free Play in the Block Center

Maurice and Sami sit near one another while working on their own constructions. They glance at each other's activity and creation from time to time, but there is little interaction. Each boy has a pile of wooden unit blocks next to him, from which he selects blocks to add to his design. They each run out of the small triangular blocks at the same time and head to the shelf to retrieve more. There are only five left, and both Sami and Maurice want all of them. Having experienced similar dilemmas in the past, and recalling the several times they have been walked through the problem-solving process with their teacher's guidance, the boys initiate the process themselves. "I need them all because my garage won't be balanced," asserts Maurice.

"But I need to finish my roof," counters Sami.

After a brief and heated discussion, they decide to split the blocks evenly but discover that this leaves one extra unit. Maurice offers to let Sami have the leftover triangle block in exchange for a long flat board that Sami has in his pile. The boys agree, and the problem is resolved.

This is an enormous accomplishment for these five-year-olds! Without previous teacher guidance, it is unlikely that the two boys would have figured out how to reach this resolution. This free-play situation, in which their teacher was not involved, provided Sami and Maurice the opportunity and motive to practice their problem-solving skills and experience the reward of their own success.

OBSERVE AND LEARN:
Mrs. Jones Sets Up Guided Play

Mrs. Jones knows that learning to share materials is an important goal for the young three-year-olds in her class. With that in mind, she plans for free play at a playdough table with four chairs. She equips the table with enough playdough for each of the four children and provides tools that can be used with the playdough; however, she intentionally provides only three of each tool: rolling pins, pizza cutters, and the popular heart-shaped cookie cutters.

Mrs. Jones has set up the playdough table to ensure that the children will bump into the need to share as they play. In anticipation, she is prepared to encourage and support the children in coming up with solutions to the problems presented by the limited resources.

OBSERVE AND LEARN:
Negotiation in the Mud Kitchen

Mr. Robbins's four-year-olds enjoy playing in the mud kitchen on the playground. When the mud kitchen was first created, it was equipped with a play stove, refrigerator, and sink, as well as a wide variety of pots, pans, stirring and scooping utensils, bowls, and mud. Children initially concentrated their attention on exploring the various tools and equipment (not to mention the mud!) and experimenting with what they could do with them. Soon, they moved beyond this exploratory stage to engage in shared pretend scenarios. This collaborative play quickly led to children having different ideas about what should occur in the mud kitchen. Will it be a pizza shop today, a family's household kitchen, a cupcake bakery, or a place for making medicine? If it is a pizza shop, who will make the dough? Will the toppings be leaves, acorns, or sand? Who will deliver the pizzas?

The children have, of course, previously encountered situations in which compromise was needed. During their play in the mud kitchen, they practice—with varying degrees of success—their capacities for negotiation. Free play offers these children the opportunity to consolidate, practice, and refine what they have been learning in more teacher-involved situations.

The Language and Literacy Domain: Building Vocabulary

Researchers David Dickinson and Joy Moreton demonstrated that the amount of time young preschoolers spend talking with one another during pretend play is predictive of the size of their vocabulary later when they are in kindergarten. Greater vocabulary development enables children to think in expanded ways about new concepts they are learning, and research shows that preschoolers' vocabulary predicts their reading comprehension in elementary school. This is a significant connection. After all, understanding what we read is the ultimate purpose of reading.

OBSERVE AND LEARN:
Miss Tiana's Class Cooks Tamales

A small group of children is playing "tamale factory" under a sheltering bush on the playground. This play theme has been popular among the children in Miss Tiana's class ever since Teo and Josefina talked about their *abuelas*, or grandmothers, making tamales for the *año nuevo*, 3or new year, celebration.

Both children have happily helped with the process at home. In their play, the children wrap dirt inside large fallen leaves and then "sell" them at a nearby workbench. Miss Tiana had observed the children's interest in making and selling, so she provided pretend money and plastic-rectangle credit cards for the children to use.

This group, composed of both native English speakers and native Spanish-speaking dual language learners, naturally exchanges vocabulary lessons in English and Spanish, learning the words *tamale, credit card, grandmother, abuela, money, dinero,* and *cornhusk*, as well as such phrases as *Happy New Year* and *Feliz Año Nuevo.*

Because the play context is highly motivating, children want to participate in this interesting and fun experience. This desire makes the children ripe and ready for learning words that help them to be part of the process of the play. The presence of physical objects in the play, as well as the shared experience of the recent new year holiday, support the acquisition of new vocabulary for all of the children.

OBSERVE AND LEARN:
Growing Gardening Vocabulary

As part of a thematic unit on gardening, Ms. Katie has introduced some new vocabulary words through picture books: *trowel, watering can, seed, shovel, soil, hand rake, moisture, sow, seedling,* and *tend*. She adds some of these real items or safer replicas to a soil table available during center time. As children incorporate these objects and substances into their play at the table, Ms. Katie models use of the new words as opportunities arise. Children begin to incorporate the new words into their play as well.

Because Terrence has a hearing impairment and reads lips to understand communication, Ms. Katie is careful to face Terrence so that his view of her mouth is unobstructed. She has set up the rectangular soil table so that children can stand on either side of it and see one another clearly. As she has done since the beginning of the year, she reminds the other children to look at Terrence's face when they talk to him.

In this play situation, all children have the opportunity to learn new vocabulary. They also have the opportunity to learn about being sensitive and responsive to the individual needs of their peers.

The Mathematical Domain: Classification

During the preschool years, children develop and practice their ability to classify objects—as well as sounds, tastes, and ideas—according to traits they have in common. Classification involves comparing, contrasting, and grouping. Classification skills are critical building blocks for learning other important mathematical concepts later on.

OBSERVE AND LEARN:
Sorting Stones

Mrs. Jones provides lots of interesting, small polished stones in a basket on the rug and invites the attention of a small group of children. She comments that the smooth, shiny stones differ from each other: Some are big, and some are small. Some contain the color red, and some do not. Some are darker, and some are lighter. Mrs. Jones provides small wooden bowls and encourages the children to use them to sort the stones in their own ways, saying, "I wonder how you could group these stones. One way is to put the bigger stones in one dish and the smaller ones in another. How else could you group them?"

She responds to what the children do with the activity. For example, "Najwa, I see you put all of the stones that sparkle in one group." "Carolina, look at what Geri did. What do you notice?" "James, tell me about the three groups you made." "I see Audrey has a different idea: She is lining up stones from smallest to largest."

In this example of teacher-guided play, Mrs. Jones introduces the concept and action of sorting as one way of playing with the stones. As the children pick up on this way of playing, Mrs. Jones supports their play with carefully chosen comments and questions.

This week, the sandbox is well equipped with a variety of transportation and construction vehicles. Jason, who has been especially interested in the books about trucks that the teacher has read over the past few days, begins to line up the vehicles. On one side of the sandbox, he lines up the construction vehicles; on the other side, he lines up the nonconstruction vehicles. Later, he brings all the vehicles back together, lining up all of the cars on one side and all of the trucks on the other. This leaves him with a small collection of vehicles that don't seem to fit in either category. He decides to line up these leftovers on a third side of the sandbox.

Through his free play, Jason is exploring and consolidating his knowledge about transportation vehicles. He is also exercising his ability to classify and reclassify objects in a variety of ways.

Physical Development and Well-Being

The time children spend outdoors is at an all-time historic low. Research suggests that the reasons for this include the lure of electronic media, parental fears about safety, and educational policies with a narrow focus on teaching academic skills through didactic methods. Outdoor physical play is important, as it provides children with benefits that cannot be readily provided through other means. Vigorous physical activity helps to prevent obesity. It increases lung function; contributes to muscle, bone, and joint health; and strengthens the heart. Vigorous physical play also increases the flow of oxygen-rich blood to the brain, which benefits brain function.

The children in Ms. Smith's class look forward to their time on the playground. With a wide variety of things to do, many children quickly and eagerly engage in riding trikes, climbing, running, and swinging. Some of the children in Ms. Smith's class gravitate toward the books displayed on a cozy blanket spread under a shade tree. Others make a beeline for the sandbox, the hay bales, the cement tunnel, or the dirt area—settings where they typically enjoy digging, hiding, talking, and pretending. Ms. Smith views outdoor time as consisting mostly of free play, and the children handle this freedom rather easily in the outdoor environment.

Ms. Smith has noticed that Brian, who has increasing difficulty attending and being still toward midmorning, seems to be rejuvenated and better able to attend to and participate in more sedentary activities following the rambunctious and loud play he is able to enjoy outside. Ms. Smith has noticed that Rhiannon, who also has difficulty with attention, becomes more focused after a period of lounging on the blanket under the tree and watering the flowers in the garden.

Although most of the children's time outdoors is spent in free play, Ms. Smith also provides opportunities for guided play. For example, to encourage those children who do not typically select vigorous play on their own, Ms. Smith invites them into brief games several times a week, including relay races, duck-duck-goose, and an obstacle course. To encourage those children who generally select only very high-energy activities, she invites them several times a week into activities such as collecting and sorting acorns and pinecones, watering the garden, or "painting" the cement wall with cans of water and large paint brushes.

Even when they are not involved in vigorous large motor activities, just being outside provides physical health benefits to children. Medical research suggests that digging in the dirt may contribute to strengthening children's immune systems and that being in sunlight not only benefits vitamin D production, which can aid building strong bones, but may also prevent the development of nearsightedness (Bell, Wilson, and Liu, 2008; Shaw, 2005; Rose et al., 2008; Lovasi et al., 2008; Misra et al., 2008). Research also suggests that playing outdoors, especially in natural settings such as grassy areas with trees and bushes rather than settings with paved surfaces devoid of vegetation, seems to have a calming effect on most children, including those with symptoms of ADHD (Taylor and Kuo, 2009; Taylor, Kuo, and Sullivan, 2001).

Self-regulation refers to young children's growing ability to control their behavior, emotions, and even parts of their thinking without relying completely on external regulation by an adult. Self-regulation is a strong predictor of children's readiness for kindergarten.

Think back to the scenario on page 9, in which children were playing tamale factory. The same basic element that made this play episode a good experience for vocabulary development also makes it a useful experience for the development of self-regulation. The experience is fun and engaging for the children; thus, the children are motivated to do what it takes to maintain the play. A big part of doing so requires regulating their own behavior to conform to the parameters of the play. For example, a child should optimally resist the impulse to suddenly throw all of the tamales in the air and proclaim—without consulting the other players—that a tornado has hit. This action is likely to disrupt the play, to cause conflict, and perhaps to make the play fall apart and no longer be a source of fun engagement. The desire to have fun while playing helps motivate children to learn to avoid such impulsive actions.

OBSERVE AND LEARN:
Simon Says

The children in Miss Morgan's preschool class enjoy the classic circle-time game Simon Says. The leader (in this case, Miss Morgan) instructs the children to engage in physical behaviors, such as "put your hands on your head," "jump up and down," "touch your nose," and so on. The tricky part is that players are supposed to follow a command only when it is begun with the words "Simon says." The game becomes even more challenging as the pace becomes faster. Children must attend, listen for "Simon says," and inhibit the impulse to follow every command they hear.

Games such as Simon Says are fun for children and provide valuable practice in using focused attention and controlling impulses. In this teacher-guided example, Miss Morgan introduces the game for the purpose of teaching self-regulation skills. Later, the children can initiate this game on their own.

Imagination and Creativity: Symbolic and Flexible Thinking

Imagination and creativity are increasingly seen as crucial tools for thriving in a future likely to be characterized by rapid technological and social change. Young children seem to have natural tendencies to be out-of-the-box thinkers, and the early childhood years are an important time to protect and nurture children's capacities for imagination and creativity.

OBSERVE AND LEARN:
Creative Repurposing through Guided Play

At a center choice table, Mrs. Gonzalez provides a group of children with small animal and human figures and a collection of found items: bottle caps, rubber jar rings, paper clips, various types of Styrofoam and plastic packing materials, metal washer disks of various sizes, and so on. Mrs. Gonzalez challenges the children to think of different things that the assorted found items could represent. She provides a couple of ideas of her own saying, "Look! This paperclip looks like part of a tiny trombone," and "Maybe this collection of bottle caps could be little swimming pools for the tiny piggies." She then responds to the direction in which the children take the play, capitalizing on teachable moments: "Chloe used the fabric swatches as blankets for the whole family. How interesting." "Elissa, tell us about your idea for those pill bottles." "Jonathan, it looks like you also found your very own way to use the fabric swatches." "Oh, Ramzi has another idea for piggy swimming pools: He put them all in the ice cube tray compartments."

Play and Motivation

Because the direction of play is, by most definitions of play, under the child's control, play is highly engaging for children. In both free and guided play, the children control the direction of the play—within appropriate limits of rights and safety, of course. In free play, teachers provide the environment, the freedom, and the time. In guided play, the teacher takes a more direct role in setting up a situation in which children are likely to encounter and grapple with particular concepts or skills. Both forms of play are important, and both are intrinsically motivating for young children. You will learn more about free play and guided play in chapter 2, and further examples of each will be described in chapters 3 through 8.

two

2

Understanding the Complex— and Simple—Nature of Play

Children play. All over the world, children play. They do not need to be forced or coaxed into playing. They will play in the absence of things that are typically considered toys and will find innovative ways to use a stick, a dirt pile, a doorstop, or their toes as playthings. They may even play with no object at all and simply imagine a plaything's existence. They may play alone, with other children, or with an adult. Play is in the nature of human beings, especially young human beings. Children play, and it is a very good thing that they do!

Play is a pleasurable activity that contributes to children's learning and development in very important ways. Because play is enticing, generally fun, and an excellent process and context for children's learning, play adds great value to early childhood education. Unlike eating food loaded with added sugar, playing is not something adults need to restrict from children. Unlike eating broccoli or spinach, we do not need to persuade them. What a lucky break! Something children want to do is actually good for them!

Defining Play

Let's look at the question "What is play?" We can potentially respond from a variety of perspectives, including researchers' views. At first, it may seem odd to think that there are scientists who study play. The phenomenon called play has been studied over many years by scholars from a variety of fields including anthropology, ethology, sociology, psychology, medicine, and education. To an extent, the description of play depends on whom you ask. Oddly, although play has been studied for a long time, a single definition of play is elusive.

Few authors writing about play would be brave enough to profess a final definition of play.

—JO AILWOOD

Play is a function of living, but it is not susceptible to exact definition . . .
the play concept remains distinct from all other forms of thought in which we express the structure of mental and social life.

—JOHAN HUIZINGA

It is interesting that while most people (including young children) know this thing called play when they see it, it is still not possible to adequately pin it down with a single definition. This highlights the multifaceted nature of play. Rather than being a simple category of behavior, play is complex. However, education researchers have proposed some defining characteristics that are generally supported.

Play...

- is enjoyable.
- is spontaneous.
- involves active participation.
- is intrinsically motivated.
- is voluntary.
- is symbolic.
- is free of external rules.
- is dominated by the players.
- is meaningful.
- is episodic.
- involves suspension of reality.

Let's explore that list a bit more to understand children's play. Play is enjoyable, which means it is generally fun. Children like to play. When an activity is basically unpleasant for a child, it is not play. Play has no extrinsic goals; it is voluntarily carried out for the intrinsic pleasure of doing it. Children play because they want to engage in the process. If a child engages in an activity primarily for the sake of gaining an external reward, the activity is not play. Play is its own reward. Play is characterized by active engagement by the child. Simply listening to a story or watching a demonstration, for example, certainly may be valuable activities. However, because the child is not actively engaged, these activities are not play. Children's active involvement in play often leads to deep engrossment in the activity.

Play often includes an element of make-believe. Although make-believe is carried out as if it were in some way real, the player understands that it is not. The poker chips transformed into coins are not literally money. Suspension of reality allows a small child in a firefighter's hat to be a six-foot-tall hero. It is understood that a child making chopping motions at the base of a tree is not really chopping it down; the action is symbolic.

Play is dominated by the players. Children decide the direction the play will take. Even though play may be governed by rules or expectations of some sort, they are expectations the children create or agree to. Play is free of externally imposed rules. Adults do not tell the players how or what to play, although they may offer suggestions or guidance or may intervene to maintain safety. You can see evidence of these characteristics of play in the example that follows.

OBSERVE AND LEARN:
Carly and Her Castle

Three-year-old Carly is busy in the block center. She lines up the small, square unit blocks, laying them flat and arranging them to form an enclosure. She places each block purposefully, being careful to create straight edges. After the rectangular construction is complete, she says to herself, "Now there gots to be the door," as she removes one of the blocks to make an opening. "The mom and babies live here, coming home," she chatters quietly to herself.

She places small dollhouse figures inside the enclosure and then moves them about for a few moments while humming. Suddenly Carly pops up and goes to a shelf to get a basket of small, decorative architectural blocks—arches, turrets, columns, and so on. She stacks several more unit blocks on the enclosure and tops them off with the architectural blocks, saying, "Well, yes, it's the queen. Her girls and her need a nice castle. Princesses. . . princessssssssses. . . princey princesses." Carly cocks her head to the side with a small smile as she lays several of the figures down. "Now, bedtime princesses."

Play and Motivation

No one told Carly to use the blocks to make an enclosure. On her own initiative, she decided what the structure would represent and what it would look like. She is thoroughly involved in her activity, and it has her rapt attention. She is not watching someone else make a castle and create a story—instead she is actively engaged in doing this. Carly is pretending. The blocks are not really a castle, the dolls are not really royalty, and she knows this. Her make-believe activity involves a private reality: Carly's own ideas and fantasy about what goes on among queens and princesses in castles. Carly's play has no extrinsic goals; the goal is the play process itself. Her purpose in this activity is not to obtain something, such as a sticker or approval or even a finished product to take home. The pleasure of the activity is its own goal. She is just playing. Or, to say it differently, "Wow! She is playing!"

Types of Play

Play comes in many forms. When you see young children engaged in playing, what you see may be object play, construction play, pretend play, rough-and-tumble play, games with rules, and often some combination of those happening all at once. The world of children's play is rich, varied, and complex.

- **Object play:** child acts upon objects to find out what they can do

- **Construction play:** child creates or builds something to represent another thing

- **Pretend play:** requires suspension of reality as a child lets an object, idea, person, or action represent something else

- **Solitary pretend play:** child engages alone in pretend play

- **Sociodramatic play:** a type of pretend play in which two or more children engage together in pretense with a shared goal

- **Games with rules:** competition between individuals or teams that is regulated by either longstanding rules or temporary agreement

- **Rough-and-tumble play:** characterized by running, chasing, fleeing, wrestling, jumping, play hitting, smiling, and laughter

Robin is engaged in object play. He is manipulating the cubes to see what he can make them do. He is not simply exploring the nature of the objects themselves; he is experimenting with how he can act upon them. If, in Robin's mind, the cubes are representing crashing race cars, then his play is also pretend play. Although he is not taking on a role himself, he is making one object (a cube) represent another (a car).

Shaquan and Omar are engaged in construction play. They have used objects (blocks, in this case) in such a way that the objects are transformed into something else. There is also an element of object play involved, as the boys have explored what they can do with the blocks. If the boys are imagining that the construction they are building is a shelter of some sort and perhaps that they are hiding from zombies, then they are not only engaging in construction play—they are also engaged in pretend play.

OBSERVE AND LEARN:
Sam, Chelsea, and a Lunch Box

Sam and Chelsea are in the dramatic play center. As Sam dons a red cape, Chelsea reminds, "Don't forget to take your lunch box, dear. There's potatoes and a corn." She extends a plastic lunch box toward Sam, who draws back and says with disgust, "Super guys don't eat corn and potatoes. I have super powers to get chicken nuggets whenever I get hungry."

Chelsea frowns and shakes her head, saying, "Well, okay. I have to go to work." She picks up a purse and stomps out of the dramatic play area.

There are several types of pretend. The type of play in which Sam and Chelsea are engaged is the most complex form of pretend play. They each take on roles and coordinate a play scenario—sociodramatic play. They are enlisting an object or action or person to symbolize another object or action or person. Sam is pretending he is a superhero; he and his red cape are standing for an "actual" superhero. Chelsea is pretending there are potatoes and corn in the lunch box. Chelsea is representing herself as an employed person as she walks off with her purse to go to her imaginary workplace.

OBSERVE AND LEARN:

Karina and Jihyun Try a Game with Rules

Karina and Jihyun, two older preschoolers, have pulled out the Candy Land game and are moving their pieces along the path as they draw cards according to the rules they have been taught. "Let's make a new rule that the blue cards really mean red!" suggests Karina. "Okay!" replies Jihyun. They continue the game using this new rule, until the two girls agree that it is too hard to remember. They then revert to the manufacturer's rules.

Games with rules are a bit different from other types of play, because the games are guided by explicit requirements. However, even in play that includes rule-governed games, the rules are under the control of the players. If players agree to the rules, whether they are original or revised or invented, this activity is considered to be play. Games with rules become common after the ages of six or seven, but some preschool children enjoy playing games with rules.

OBSERVE AND LEARN:
Austin, Marco, and Samir
Engage in Rough-and-Tumble Play

Austin, Marco, and Samir are thoroughly engrossed as they run around on the playground with a great display of energy, whooping and hollering and knocking each other down. They make crashing noises as they tumble on the ground, then pick themselves up and resume running.

Observation of the boys' facial expressions and tone of voice reveals that there is no real anger involved in this activity. The boys are play fighting rather than engaging in actual aggression. Because this kind of play can look like aggression on its surface, many teachers may be uncomfortable with rough-and-tumble play. This kind of play is important to the development of self-regulation and emotional awareness and may be especially so for boys. The contributions of rough-and-tumble play, and suggestions for managing it safely, are presented in later chapters.

Free Play and Guided Play

We've seen that play may be solitary or social. It can also be freely chosen and governed by the children or guided by an adult. In the examples so far, children initiated the play. The children decided what to play with and how to play with it. The children in each of these scenarios controlled the direction of the play. Karina and Jihyun, for example, chose the Candy Land game from among a variety of other options. They could have chosen to play another board game, to draw at the journal table, or to build at the block center. They controlled the way they played the game, alternating between the original rules they had learned and a modified rule they invented. Free play is play in which children choose what to play with and how to play, with little or no intervention from an adult.

Guided play is a bit different. Let's imagine that Shaquan and Omar's construction play with the large hollow blocks began like this:

Ms. Jenkins sits down with Omar and Shaquan after calling them over to the outdoor block area on the patio. She wonders aloud whether they can build a bridge that's big enough for both of them to sit under. The two boys rise to the challenge with enthusiasm.

While consulting with one another, they stack three rectangular blocks end on end, and three more end on end about 2 feet away from the first stack. The two stacks of blocks are quite high and precarious. Ms. Jenkins observes, "Wow, looks wobbly. Is this going to work?"

"Yes!" proclaims Omar.

As the boys lay a plank across the two stacks of blocks, the construction comes tumbling down. "I know," says Shaquan. "Let's do it this way." He lays a rectangular block on the floor so that its largest face is flush against the carpet, then he stacks another on it in the same way.

"What are you thinking?" asks Ms. Jenkins.

"This way is stronger," says Omar. The boys then complete a sturdy bridge and sit under it together.

Ms. Jenkins asks, "So, how did you lay the blocks to make the bridge stronger?"

"We put this part onto the floor," says Shaquan, pointing to the largest face of one of the blocks.

"What part is that?" asks Ms. Jenkins.

"The big part," says Shaquan.

"The biggest part," says Omar.

In this version of Shaquan and Omar's construction play, the teacher has initiated the play. She has offered a challenge to the boys with a goal in mind—constructing a sufficiently sturdy bridge that is large enough to arch over two boys. Ms. Jenkins has in mind several principles of geometry and mechanics that the boys' play will support. As the play unfolds, largely under the direction of the children, Ms. Jenkins takes advantage of opportunities to support the boys' learning through her brief comments and questions.

Guided play is initiated by an adult with potential learning goals in mind but unfolds mainly through the children's choices during the play. The adult may provide support throughout the process to move a child toward achieving potential goals.

In an early childhood classroom, both free play and guided play involve a teacher. However, the teacher's role is different in these two kinds of play, as illustrated in the table that follows.

Types of Activity

TYPE	ADULT DIRECTED	CHILD DIRECTED
Adult Initiated	Not play	Guided play
Child Initiated	Not play	Free play

Adapted from Weisberg, Deena, et al. 2015. "Making Play Work for Education."
Phi Delta Kappan 96(8): 8–13.

As the table demonstrates, free play and guided play differ in terms of who initiates the play. Free play is initiated by the child, for the child's own purposes. Guided play is initiated by the adult, who has potential learning goals for the child in mind. Both types of play are directed by the child; in other words, the child has control of the direction the play takes. Beyond the initiation, the adult's role differs in these two types of play. In free play, the adult's role is to occasionally respond to the child's play and to intervene only when issues of safety and rights are at stake. In guided play, the adult provides support to increase the likelihood that the child will reach the potential learning that the adult has in mind. Let's examine a few more examples of guided play.

OBSERVE AND LEARN:
Sharing in the Kitchen Area

Ms. Janie has equipped the play kitchen with a variety of real pots, pans, and cooking utensils. She has intentionally provided duplicates of some items but not of others. Ms. Janie has done this because one of the children in her class, Clara, needs support with learning to take turns. Clara has Down syndrome with cognitive delays and loves to play in the kitchen. When Ms. Janie sees Clara enter the kitchen area where Ellen and Anthony are playing, she moves in closer to watch the play. She suggests, "Maybe the three of you could be chefs in a restaurant and prepare a big feast by working together. What could your jobs be?"

As the three children choose roles and carry them out, Ms. Janie sees an opportunity: Clara wants the eggbeater and large metal bowl that Anthony is using, and she grabs them. There is another large metal bowl available but only one eggbeater. Ms. Janie prompts Anthony and Clara to each voice their concerns while she holds the eggbeater. She encourages them to consider solutions. Ultimately, the children decide that Clara will use the large wooden spoon while Anthony finishes beating his pretend eggs. They also agree that Anthony will trade with Clara when he is finished.

In this example, Ms. Janie has purposefully created a context for conflict resolution and has intentionally provided support for both Anthony and Clara to practice turn-taking skills.

OBSERVE AND LEARN:
Width, Height, and Shape at the Playdough Table

Mrs. Ferguson has been planning activities for her four- and five-year-olds, focusing on size and shape. She decides to equip the playdough table with a variety of 1-cup measures in different shapes and dimensions. Although the shapes and dimensions differ—squared or rounded, tall and narrow, short and wide—each container holds the same volume, 8 ounces. She prepares the playdough table in this way to maximize the likelihood that children will notice and think about shape, height, and width. She also aims to maximize the possibility that some children will engage with the concept of conservation, which is the fact that the volume of a substance remains the same no matter how you shape it, as long as none of the substance is taken away.

As the children interact with the materials, Mrs. Ferguson asks intermittent questions such as, "Which of these cups is taller?" "Which is wider?" "Do you think this one will hold more playdough than this one?" "How could you find out?" "Did these three hold the same amount?" "How do you know?" Of course, Mrs. Ferguson does not barrage the children with a long list of questions. Instead, she allows them time to explore and play on their own, while watching their activity attentively and occasionally providing interested commentary: "I see you filled them both to the top."

In this scenario, the children still lead the play, and Mrs. Ferguson responds in ways that enhance the chances that children will "bump into" the learning goals she has in mind. She has guided the children toward an opportunity to play with concepts of size, shape, and volume.

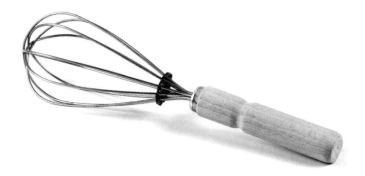

OBSERVE AND LEARN:
Matching Animal Pictures with Their Beginning Letters

Mr. Jason has noticed that the children usually choose to play with the matching animal picture cards either by sorting them into categories of animals and letters or by lining up the cards to make an animal parade. While

these are both valuable experiences, he wants to introduce the children to another way to use the cards. The class has recently been focusing on initial sounds, mostly through reading books and looking at pictures. Mr. Jason calls Jack over to the table and says, "I want to show you another way to use these cards. What is this animal?"

Jack says, "A monkey!"

Mr. Jason says, "Monkey. In this pile of letters, can you find the letter for the first sound in monkey? Listen carefully. What is the first sound in m-m-m-monkey?"

"Mmm," replies Jack.

Mr. Jason asks, "Can you find the letter that makes the sound /mmm/?" Jack finds the card with the letter M and continues the activity this way on his own. Mr. Jason shows his interest in Jack's activity through encouraging comments such as, "You found it!" and by asking helpful questions such as, "What is the name of the letter you are looking for?" When Jack loses interest after several minutes, he is free to play with the cards in another way.

In each of these examples, the teacher has provided some structure to the activity, through forethought about materials to provide, how to introduce the activity, or how to provide support in a way that maximizes chances that the children will practice and move toward one or more particular learning goals.

Both free play and guided play are important to young children's development and learning. In each of the situations described, the teacher could have taken a less direct role and allowed the children to engage in free play. The children would likely have had positive experiences during that free play, contributing in important ways to their long-term learning and development. They may or may not, however, have practiced the particular skills or explored the specific concepts in which they engaged through adult guidance.

Children Want to Play

Play is an activity in which children engage willingly. That characteristic alone makes it a powerful process for learning. They want to play! They may engage in play alone, with a partner, or with several others. Their play may involve object play, construction play, pretend play, rough-and-tumble play, games with rules, or a combination of these. Each of these types of play may occur as guided play or as free play. Virtually all young children engage in play, including young children who have disabilities. Children with disabilities may play in different ways from other children. Children with disabilities may sometimes need different kinds of support for their play; however, their play is as equally important as the play of children who are typically developing.

three 3

Understanding the Teacher's Roles as Children Play

For play to reach its full power as a learning experience for children, there is more for a teacher to do than simply allowing it to happen. Early childhood teachers can and should use a variety of strategies to support children's play. These strategies depend upon the nature of a child's play in a particular situation and the learning goals that the teacher is seeking to support at a given time. Effective teachers are aware of a wide variety of strategies and are able to select and use them with intentionality, whether they are responding to children's spontaneous free play, initiating and guiding a guided play experience, or using other nonplay learning formats such as whole group, small group, or routines.

Intentional early childhood teachers exhibit the following qualities:

- Thoughtfulness

- Purposefulness

- Good planning

- Awareness of important program goals

- Knowledge of developmentally appropriate practice

- Recognition of teachable moments

- Ability to make informed, on-the-spot decisions

Intentional teachers make purposeful plans and quick decisions about learning formats, teaching strategies, age-appropriate group goals, and goals for individual children.

Effective teachers are intentional in virtually all that they do. Intentionality involves thoughtfulness and purposefulness. In being intentional, good teachers are aware of important goals for children and direct their thoughtful planning and decision making to the purpose of progressing toward those goals. This is no less true with regard to play than with other early learning activities.

In their book *Developmentally Appropriate Practice in Early Childhood Programs Serving Children from Birth through Age Eight*, researchers Carol Copple and Sue Bredekamp sum up these ideal characteristics: "In everything that good teachers do—creating the environment, considering the curriculum and tailoring it to the children as individuals, planning learning experiences, and interacting with children and families—they are purposeful and thoughtful. As they make myriad decisions, big and small, they keep in mind the outcomes they seek. Even in responding to unexpected opportunities—'teachable moments'—intentional teachers are guided by the outcomes the program is trying to help children reach and by their knowledge of child development and learning."

Before the play, the teacher is acting in a planning role and can focus on the following:

- Important goals for children's learning
- Providing provocations
- Providing time and space
- Helping children make plans and choices
- Providing materials

During the play, the teacher acts as a guide, exhibiting the following behaviors:

- Being a supportive presence
- Suggesting ideas
- Inviting
- Adding materials
- Describing
- Modeling
- Paraphrasing
- Demonstrating
- Responding
- Adding challenge
- Encouraging
- Simplifying
- Questioning
- Providing information
- Interpreting

After the play, the teacher supports children's learning from the experience in the following ways:

- Documenting and reflecting
- Encouraging reflection and representation by children
- Displaying documentation

Recall the difference between free play and guided play. Adult-directed activity, while it is an important and necessary part of any early childhood program, is not play. Play activity is always directed by the child. Play activity that is initiated by the child and directed by the child is free play. Play activity that is initiated by the teacher but directed by the child is guided play.

Although free play and guided play are different, both are important. Teachers do provide support for both kinds of play, and sometimes the kinds of support they provide are similar. In both free play and guided play, teachers plan in advance. In free play, it is possible that children will not need any support beyond what you do in your planning roles. However, teachable moments will often emerge during free play, so teachers may also use strategies for guiding play during a free-play episode. It requires judgment to decide whether to stay out and observe or to step in and draw out a teachable moment. In free play, many teachers step in only when there is a possibility of harm to a child or serious infringement on a child's rights requiring guidance with conflict resolution. In guided play, your role is to set up the play to encourage children to engage with a particular goal but then respond to where the children take it. Otherwise, the activity loses the essence of play.

Before Play: Acting as Planner

Effective early childhood teachers are intentional in their planning for children's play. They think carefully about how goals may be met. They arrange the daily schedule and the physical environment purposefully, to encourage and support play and learning. They choose materials not for their entertainment value but for their potential to engage children and move them toward important outcomes. As they consider learning outcomes, teachers may also create a variety of interesting ways to spark children's play ideas.

Be aware of important goals for children's learning and development. Programs for young children have purposes beyond keeping children safe and occupied for a specified period of time each day. As you plan for play, your knowledge of early childhood development and important developmental processes in the early years should guide you. All states in the United States have created early learning standards for children ages three to five, which describe important learning and developmental goals. The National Association for the Education of Young Children (NAEYC) is an excellent source of information about developmentally appropriate goals for early childhood, as are a variety of textbooks on early childhood development and curriculum. Let's look at some outcome goals and how a teacher may plan in advance to support children's movement toward those goals through play.

Provide Time for Play

High-quality play, which helps to move children toward important learning goals, does not usually occur within brief periods of play time. It takes sustained time for children to develop complex play episodes, especially pretend and construction play. When children are allowed only fifteen or twenty minutes to play, the allotted time is ending just as the play really gets going! Imagine how frustrating that can be. When children realize that this is the norm, they may lose their motivation to get started in pretend and construction play in the first place.

So, how much time do preschool children need for play? The answer to that question seems to depend on the particular group of children and the time of year. Children with a lot of play experience may be able to launch right in to quality play. On the other hand, less-experienced children and children new to a particular class may need time to sample and explore the possibilities offered by a center or by the classroom as a whole, before they can become deeply engaged in play. One study by researchers James Christie and Francis Wardle found that it took at least thirty minutes for children to begin to engage in complex play. Others, such as Marjorie Kostelnik et al. and NAEYC, have suggested a time block of forty-five to sixty minutes be allotted for freely chosen play.

Because good play takes time, it is important to think about the way that time is organized. Some teachers use a system of center rotation, in which small groups of children spend ten or fifteen minutes at a center and are then required to rotate to another center and then to a third and perhaps a fourth. Fifteen minutes may be sufficient for play with manipulatives or for drawing with markers at the writing center. For many children, however, it may be more time than they are comfortable with for engaging with fine-motor and eye-hand–coordination tasks. They may tire after that much time and engage in disruptive behavior as a result. Conversely, fifteen minutes in the block center, pretend play center, or the book center is not likely to be enough for many children. They are unlikely to even begin to be deeply engaged in pretend or construction play after ten or fifteen minutes. It is easy to see how requiring a child to close a book when the timer rings can be frustrating.

Some teachers allow children to make their own choices with regard to how much time they will spend engaged in a particular play activity. Other teachers provide a time of day during which children can make their own choices about time and provide another time of day that is more structured.

Provide Materials for Play

In the following wet sand examples, Ms. Katrina does not haphazardly grab a bunch of toys from a shelf. She does not limit the materials to a particular set of containers and scoops just because "that is what we always use." Instead, she is thoughtful about the role of materials in children's learning through play. She chooses to provide wet sand rather than dry because this would enable the children to invert their measuring cups to create "cakes" that could then be further compared for size. She includes actual feeding spoons and a baby doll knowing that Farah, who has developmental delays, needs practice with the fine-motor skills involved in self-feeding. She includes a variety of kitchen toys because she knows many children like to engage in social pretend play involving food preparation. She provides a small table right next to the sand table to create extra space; this allows her to offer a greater number of sand toys without overcrowding the sand table itself. In addition, she selects materials to accommodate a variety of developmental needs and intentionally excludes such toys as cars and trucks, which would likely have required a lot of space and have infringed upon the measuring, filling, spooning, "cooking," and other opportunities provided at this small indoor sand table.

Selecting materials is an important planning role that teachers fulfill to support children's learning through play. Consider the following factors:

- **Variety:** sufficient to support different interests, developmental levels, background experiences, types of play, and goals

- **Flexibility:** both realistic materials, such as cell phones (batteries removed) in the dramatic play center, and open-ended materials, such as cardboard packing pieces in the block or art center

- **Number and amount:** As a general rule, provide about two-and-a-half times as many objects or sets as there are children. However, sometimes provide fewer materials to encourage sharing. Consider having more than one of a highly popular toy, if sharing is too difficult for the children.

OBSERVE AND LEARN:
Wet Sand

Ms. Katrina is preparing her preschool classroom for the coming week. It has been a while since she last brought the water table into the classroom. She decides to put it in the sensory center and fill it with sand instead of water. The children have had fun with the sand table in the past and have remained engaged for long periods of time. Ms. Katrina decides that the sand table will be a center choice option. Although she intends for the children to play at the sand table in their own ways, Ms. Katrina is aware of a wide variety of long-term educational goals that can potentially be facilitated through sand play. As she sets up the center, she thinks about these important goals.

Sand play can support learning goals in a variety of areas, such as mathematics, vocabulary, oral language, social skills, fine-motor skills, and science. In *Developmentally Appropriate Curriculum*, author Marjorie Kostelnik and colleagues identified some ways to use sand play to address long-term goals:

- Develop a mathematics vocabulary to describe *quantity, equality, inequality,* and *relative amount.*

- Use speaking abilities to articulate ideas, intents, emotions, and desires.

- Develop social skills such as knowing and using people's names.

- Negotiate conflicts in peaceful ways by compromising, bargaining, and standing up for their own and others' rights.

- Understand measurable attributes of objects and units, systems, and processes of measurement by using nonstandard and standard tools.

- Coordinate wrist, hand, finger, finger-thumb, and eye-hand movements.

- Use tools skillfully, including implements for eating, writing, dressing, and playing.

Because she has taken a few moments to consider some of the many possible long-term goals that can be facilitated by playing at the sand table, Ms. Katrina is mentally prepared to notice children's behavior with regard to these and other possible learnings that are embedded in the sand-play opportunity. Ms. Katrina is also ready to comment in response to the children's play interactions.

During Play: Acting as Observer and Facilitator

Teachers' roles during children's play include the following strategies:

- **Observe:** As a play-support strategy, observation is an essential tool to help you decide which other strategies, if any, to use in a particular play situation. Observation is an invaluable form of data collection. You may use your observations and your interpretations of those observations to make on-the-spot decisions about how best to immediately support children's play. You may also use your observations for later decision making about how you might structure a child's future play opportunities. Decisions about how to guide children's play are based on your knowledge of important goals, your knowledge of the individual children involved, and your observation of the present situation. In the following example, Ms. Osborn's carefully attuned observations and quick reflection enable her to form some good ideas about how best to support Marquis as he struggles with a challenging puzzle.

She makes a quick decision about how to intervene, with the intention that Marquis will not lose his sense of competence and his desire to persevere. She crouches down next to him, puts a hand on his shoulder, and says gently, "You look frustrated. That piece doesn't fit?"

"It won't go in," Marquis says with heated exasperation.

"Remember, sometimes you can turn it around and try it different ways," she says encouragingly. Marquis's posture begins to relax as he reorients the puzzle piece a couple of times until it fits. Ms. Osborn pats his arm and says, "You tried some different ideas, and you found how to do it!" She stays close by, maintaining a supportive presence as Marquis inserts several more pieces successfully. She says, "You're almost there! I'll come back in a couple minutes to see how you are doing." As she walks away, Ms. Osborn makes a mental note to add a couple of slightly easier puzzles for choice time in the afternoon. She plans to encourage Marquis to do puzzles again in the afternoon, and she reasons that if he chooses to do so, he can work with some easier ones that will support successful practice. He will also have the more challenging shark puzzle to tackle again if he chooses.

■ **Be a supportive presence:** In the example above, Ms. Osborn uses proximity and quiet attention in combination with several other strategies. After Marquis has calmed down and continued his efforts, she remains near and watches him. Sometimes, a teacher's supportive presence is adequate all by itself, as in the following example.

OBSERVE AND LEARN:
Helping a New Student Join In

Josue is relatively new to Mr. Matheson's class. His native language is Spanish, and he has only spoken a few words of English in the classroom so far. Josue stands watching, about 5 feet away from a table where two boys are playing with shaving cream, rubbing it across the smooth table with their hands. Mr. Matheson notices Josue observing and suspects that he wants to join the boys. Over the past several days, Mr. Matheson has helped Josue to join play by prompting him with, "You can say, 'I want to play here.'" Seeing that there is room for him at the table, Mr. Matheson decides to see if Josue can now do this on his own, with minimal support. Mr. Matheson stands close to the table. Josue looks at him, and Mr. Matheson smiles and nods his head. Josue approaches the table and says, "Play here," as he takes a seat and tentatively touches the shaving cream.

In this case, Mr. Matheson's purpose is for Josue to enter into play as independently as he is able. He stays close by and acknowledges Josue's glance, thereby providing a supportive presence.

- **Invite:** A simple invitation can often pull together children who might not otherwise have played together. In the example below, a teacher sees an opportunity to extend a child's play to a higher level of complexity by inviting another child into the play.

OBSERVE AND LEARN:
Complex Play in the Sandbox

Miss Alito is sitting on the edge of the sandbox as Victor loads a dump truck with sand then dumps it out repetitively. As Romi walks by, Miss Alito sees an opportunity to enrich Victor's sandbox play. She invites Romi into the situation by saying, "Come join us, Romi. Victor is filling this dump truck. There is another one right here."

- **Describe:** Describing out loud what you see children doing as they play can accomplish a couple of things. First, it gives children the message that you are interested in what they are doing and that you respect their play enough to notice. It also can serve to point out to children aspects of their play that they may not have noticed, leading them to think or act at a higher level.

PLANNING FOR PLAY

As the children play, Ms. Katrina notices Lamont frowning and reaching for a spoon in use by another child. "Lamont, if you want a turn with the spoon, what can you say to Bobbie?" She continues observing: "Farah, I see how carefully you are lifting the spoon of sand to feed to the baby." In reaction to Cici, who says, "I'm making birthdays!" Ms. Katrina says, "Look, Sara—Cici is getting ready for a birthday with muffins!"

Ms. Katrina jots in her observation notes, "Barry used two half-cup measures to fill the 1-cup measure, several times. Seems to be playing with idea of halves and wholes. Maybe plan follow-up activity."

Mrs. Quincy is intentionally working to provide Bradley with more opportunities for fine-motor experience. She has found some small wooden blocks and has put sticker pictures of cars on them, knowing that Bradley likes cars. She initiates play with Bradley by inviting him to the manipulatives table, showing him the new blocks. She says, "Show me how you can stack these car blocks." As she watches him stack the blocks with the broad sides down, which is the easier way, she describes his activities: "You've stacked five blocks. I see you've put them with the big side down." These simple descriptions are just meant to tell Bradley, "I notice," and "I see this." Bradley now tries, on his own, a different way to stack the blocks. He stacks them with the narrow sides down, which is the harder way, further challenging his perceptual-motor skills.

- **Encourage:** There are many ways to encourage children as they engage in play. Description, as Mrs. Quincy uses with Bradley, is one form of encouragement that communicates your interest and your valuing of children's play activities. Descriptive praise is another form of encouragement, as shown in this next example.

OBSERVE AND LEARN:
Encouraging Colors

Petra is at the journaling center, drawing in her journal notebook with markers. She is making bands of color around the edges of the page, like a frame. She has put a band of turquoise next to a band of orange. Petra's teacher sees this and says, "I see the way you put orange next to turquoise. Wow, that looks so bright and eye-catching to me! That is pretty!"

Another way to provide encouragement is to avoid messages that create competition between children and instead encourage children to self-evaluate in comparison to their own performance. For example: "I see that you finished the rainforest puzzle. Let's see, it has . . . twenty pieces! I remember when you used to do only the ten-piece puzzles. You practiced a lot, and you are getting more and more skilled with puzzles. Pat yourself on the back!"

- **Provide a challenge:** In the example with Bradley and the car blocks, Mrs. Quincy uses description, which seems to lead Bradley to challenge himself further. As a teacher, you can also enrich children's play by providing a direct challenge, as Mr. Carlson does in the following example.

OBSERVE AND LEARN:
Color Mixologists

Anaya and Amelia have been playing at the discovery center, where Mr. Carlson has provided small, white, plastic muffin pans; three baby-food jars with colored water in red, blue, and yellow; and plastic droppers. Anaya and Amelia have been haphazardly and quickly mixing up the colors, pouring them out into a receptacle in the middle of the table, and then mixing the colors again. Seeing this, Mr. Carlson steps in and provides a challenge: "Let's see how you can make the color orange. Try two colors to see if you can make orange." After a couple of tries, the girls create orange by mixing yellow and red. Mr. Carlson then provides another challenge by asking, "How could you remember that you can use yellow and red to make orange?" With his support, the girls come up with the idea of creating a color-mixing journal in which they can act as color scientists to record their discoveries about how to use the primary colors to make secondary colors.

■ **Question:** Different kinds of questions require children to think and respond in different ways. Unfortunately, many teachers limit themselves to using mostly factual questions that require either a yes-no response or a single-word correct response. Children who hear a preponderance of these kinds of questions often begin to think of questions as tests to see whether they know the right answer and consequently become disinterested in teacher questions. There are many more useful and intriguing ways to employ questioning! In the following example, Ms. Raquel uses a question that is designed to get Mari and Sangmi to examine their thinking.

OBSERVE AND LEARN:
Open-Ended Questions

Last week, Ms. Raquel conducted a group activity in which she encouraged children to predict how quickly a small car would roll down ramps with varying slopes, and she then demonstrated. She has now added a variety of ramps and materials to construct ramps to the block center to provoke children's experimentation. Mari and Sangmi are the first children to engage with the materials. They have each created a ramp and have agreed that the car will probably go faster down Mari's ramp. Before they test this theory, Ms. Raquel steps in and says, "Wait. I'm really interested in your idea. What makes you think that it will go faster on Mari's ramp? How did you think of that idea?" These questions prompt Mari and Sangmi to think about their thinking. Ms. Raquel knows that this kind of metacognitive thinking is an important aspect of cognitive development that will open the children to new kinds of learning.

Open-ended questions are used to encourage critical and creative thinking and to engage children in conversation. They have no one correct answer; they can have multiple answers. Consider, for example, "What do you like about dogs?" Closed questions are usually employed in situations in which the teacher is not trying to engage children in critical or creative thinking but rather to get a short reply to obtain specific information; for example: "What is your dog's name?" The following are selected types of open-ended questions:

- **Questions to encourage children to make comparisons:** "What is the same about these?"

- **Questions to encourage children to be aware of their own thinking:** "What made you decide to try that?" or "How do you know?"

- **Questions to encourage children to observe:** "What do you notice about this?"

- **Questions to encourage children to make predictions:** "Where do you think the marble will roll if you start it here?"

- **Questions to encourage children to make decisions:** "How would you like to do it this time?"

- **Add materials:** In the example below, Ms. Joni has encouraged higher-level play by adding a variety of materials to a center. Materials can also be added on the spot during a play episode.

OBSERVE AND LEARN:
Revitalizing Play in a Tired Center

The pretend-play center in Ms. Joni's class of three-year-olds is equipped with the basics, including a wooden refrigerator, sink, doll cradle, doll highchair, oven and stove, and table and chairs. There are pots, pans, dishes, several dolls and doll blankets, dress-up clothes for the children to wear, purses, backpacks, and cell phones.

Lately, Ms. Joni has noticed that the quality of play in this center is declining. There are more conflicts, and fewer children are choosing to go there and stay there. She has also noticed an increasing interest among the children in writing and reading activities. Children have begun to write notes—which usually just consist of scribbles—to one another at the writing center, placing them in envelopes to be delivered to cubbies. Several children have also begun to "read" aloud to stuffed animals in the book center.

After removing a few items to make more room in the pretend-play center, Ms. Joni adds a real mailbox; a small desk and chair; writing utensils, paper, and envelopes; a small rocking chair and several board books; and several wallets with "checkbooks." She introduces these changes during the morning meeting on Monday. By Friday, she notes that children are eagerly incorporating literacy materials into their play, and their play in the pretend-play center has become both happier and more complex.

Making changes to a center can entice children back to playing there, can boost the quality of their play, and can capitalize upon and support their interests.

After Play: Acting as Guide to In-Depth Learning

Sometimes, guided play grows out of what was initially a free-play experience. In the following example, Ms. Katrina plans a guided-play experience based on what she notices during the free-play time at the sand table.

OBSERVE AND LEARN:
Wet Sand (continued)

After the sand table has been available for a couple of days as a free-play option, Ms. Katrina decides to use it for guided play. Because she has noted Barry and Portia's interest in the measuring cups, she decides to guide their play toward specific, related goals. She calls them to the sand table, saying, "I've noticed you playing with these three measuring cups. This one is a whole-cup measure. This one is a half-cup measure. This one is a quarter-cup measure. I wonder if you know how many of this half-cup measure it will take to fill this whole-cup measure. Do you want to guess? How can you find out?" As the two children investigate, Ms. Katrina asks, "Which one holds more sand? Which one holds less sand?" She then repeats this series of questions with the quarter-cup measure and the half-cup measure and finishes with final challenge questions: "How many quarter-cup measures will it take to fill the whole-cup measure? How do you know? How can you find out?"

Ms. Katrina is aware of developmentally appropriate goals for the children she works with, so she has the framework to be intentional in supporting children's playful activities with regard to those goals. She was primed and ready to see the teachable moments that arose, and she responded with gentle support and encouragement. She initiated guided play in a way to draw children's attention to the measurement of volume or to mathematical vocabulary related to relative amount—such as more than and less than.

Your role in helping children learn through play is not over when the play materials have been put away! In addition to reflecting upon your own observations as a basis to plan for future play and nonplay learning experiences, you can also encourage children to reflect upon their play.

OBSERVE AND LEARN:
Documenting Play

Mr. Tate uses his cell-phone camera as a tool for supporting the play of the four- and five-year-olds in his class. He sometimes uses it to capture a sequence of images of children engaged in an especially spirited episode, for example as they participate in a high-energy game of chase on the playground. At other times, he has used the camera to document the various stages of a construction, such as the airport that Kurt, Stephen, and Malik built in the block center. Mr. Tate will sometimes print and display these photographs on a bulletin board near the gathering rug, toward the end of the same day when the play occurred. When children gather on the rug for their end-of-the-day meeting, Mr. Tate can use this photographic documentation as a way to encourage children to reflect upon their day and their play.

With or without photo documentation, children can and should be encouraged to think back about their play. This can provide ideas for future play, expanding upon children's play choices and selection of playmates. It encourages children to be intentional, to think about how experiences make them feel, and to make choices based on past experiences. Representing their experiences through speaking, drawing, and writing can help to solidify children's memories, making them more tangible and accessible. It also conveys the message that their play is valued and is important business.

Consider the following possibilities for encouraging children to reflect about their play:

- After children return from the playground, wash hands, and have a drink of water, have them sit down and draw a picture or write a word about something they played on the playground.

- At snack time, have children take a silent close-your-eyes moment to think about something they played that morning. Then, allow each child to verbally share that something with the rest of the table.

- At circle time, show children photographs of group play that you took earlier in the day. Allow the children who were involved in the photographed play to dictate something about what was happening in the photo, as you write it down.

- When transitioning from after-play circle to snack time, choose one child to pantomime something she did during play time. The other children can guess what she is representing through the pantomime.

Documentation also allows teachers to reflect on past play and plan for future play, as well as to record children's development as shown in their play. In addition to photo documentation, other means of documenting play can include brief anecdotal records describing children's play behaviors, audiotape recordings, checklists, and classroom mapping strategies to record the play areas in which individual children spend their time.

As you experiment with ways to support children's play, you will be able to use different strategies to provide different kinds and amounts of support. For example, providing materials can be considered a lower level of support; it is an indirect and minimal form of help. The same is true for providing a supportive presence. More direct strategies include modeling and providing information. Deciding what support to provide in a particular situation and to a particular child is an important decision-making role for intentional teachers. The related concepts of *scaffolding* and the *zone of proximal development* are helpful for making decisions about how much support to provide.

Psychologist Lev Vygotsky identified the zone of proximal development (ZPD) as the space between what a particular child cannot do independently and what he can do when given support from an adult or more able child. Vygotsky advocated scaffolding, which is the process of providing only as much support as the child needs to cross that zone of proximal development and accomplish the task, and then gradually withdrawing that support as the child gains the ability to ultimately achieve the task on his own.

The ZPD and the process of scaffolding are related to the importance of both mastery and challenge in children's learning. Provide too much challenge, and children can become frustrated and give up. Provide not enough challenge, and children can become bored and restless. Children need opportunities to experience challenges for which they need a little bit of support and must stretch themselves. Children need opportunities to master accomplishments that are just outside of their reach. At the same time, children also need opportunities to practice tasks that they have already mastered.

■ ■

four | 4 |

Encouraging
Social-Emotional Competence

Remember the education trend emphasizing the "whole child?" Thinking of children as whole beings reminds us that all aspects of children's learning and development are not only important but are interconnected. This is especially true of learning and development in the social and emotional domains. It can be difficult to tease out which aspects of a child's functioning are "social" and which are "emotional." Because they are so closely related, we will consider them together. The social-emotional domain has to do with the child's growing competence in areas including interpersonal skills, positive self-identity, emotional intelligence, and social values. Another aspect of social-emotional development is self-regulation, which will be discussed in chapter 5.

The Importance of Social-Emotional Competence

The abilities to interact effectively, to recognize and interpret others' feelings, and to manage our own feelings constructively are basic to our well-being and to our overall success in life. The growth of social-emotional competence is fundamentally important in its own right. While some people may think of these areas of a child's development as the responsibility solely of a child's family, the preschool setting can offer many advantages that make it a prime context for the growth of social-emotional competence. The preschool context can offer peers with whom to interact, materials that may not be present in the child's home environment, and teachers who are knowledgeable about social-emotional goals and who are skilled in supporting progress toward those goals. A good preschool setting offers protected time for children's play, which is a critically important context for the growth of social-emotional competence.

The growth of social and emotional competence is also important because it lays a foundation for children's school readiness and their achievement in further schooling. Social-emotional competence is a strong predictor of children's readiness for kindergarten and their academic success in the early grades. Children who have strong social and emotional skills also tend to have more positive attitudes toward school, higher academic motivation and achievement, and fewer absences, according to education researcher Joseph Zins and colleagues. It is quite a challenge for children to learn at school if they have difficulty getting along with others, controlling their own impulses, or expressing strong feelings in appropriate and constructive ways. The research to support this is convincing, according to psychologist C. Cybele Raver: "From the last two decades of research, it is unequivocally clear that children's emotional and behavioral adjustment is important for their chance of early school success." Subsequent research provides additional strong support.

Play as a Means to Develop Social-Emotional Competence

In play, children re-create scenarios and roles that reflect the social world in which they live. Children are often able to do and be things in the context of play before they can do and be those things in other contexts. Children can often behave in socially confident and competent ways in play before they can use these abilities as effectively outside of play.

Because play is by nature a self-motivated and highly engaging activity, children generally are motivated to act in ways that allow it to continue. Play heightens the motivation to communicate wants, to negotiate conflicts, and to take turns. For example, as children pretend to run a car wash using tricycles on the playground, the fun of the activity enhances their desire to resolve issues such as who will play which role and how to line up for the car wash.

PLANNING FOR PLAY

As children engage in pretend play, they often act out emotional situations, pretending to be happy, sad, angry, or scared. You might hear a child say, "Oh, no! We must save the babies from the fire!" These pretend scenarios provide children fruitful opportunities to use emotion-related words, to consider the causes of emotions, or to enact and "read" the facial expressions and behaviors associated with particular feelings.

Children often use play as a means of dealing with distress. For example, a child who has witnessed a devastating house fire may choose to engage in pretend scenarios as a firefighter over several days, as a way of feeling some mastery and control over her fear. She may enact the scenario to a more acceptable end, or she may repeatedly play out a sad outcome such as burying a family pet lost in the fire. Even for far less traumatic events, a child may reverse roles through play as a coping mechanism. For example, a young child who has been scolded by a parent may transform herself into the parent as she similarly scolds her beloved stuffed animal. As adults we may play out traumatic events in our heads as a means of "getting a grip" on a difficult situation. Young children quite literally play them out in action.

As a preschool teacher, you can support children's social and emotional development in many ways. General teaching and guidance practices as well as the overall organization and structure of your classroom and the curriculum materials being used influence social-emotional competence. These factors affect the emotional climate of the classroom as well as the number and types of opportunities children have for both peer and teacher-child interaction. Preschool teachers can also support social and emotional competence by using curriculum materials and activities designed for that purpose, such as social-problem-solving exercises, role-playing activities, and sharing of stories and other books. There are research-based curriculum packages available for those purposes, such as the Second Step Early Learning program and the Incredible Years program. Many of the research-supported strategies for enhancing young children's social-emotional competence are intended to be used in the context of play, as so much of children's social interaction with peers naturally occurs during playful activities.

Identifying Goals for Social-Emotional Development

During the early childhood years, children are progressing toward the achievement of a wide variety of social and emotional skills. The following list is not exhaustive but offers an overview of some important social-emotional goals for preschool children, as identified by Marjorie Kostelnik and colleagues in *Developmentally Appropriate Curriculum* and by the National Council for the Social Studies. For further information in this area, you can explore some of the references cited in this table, your state's standards for early learning, the program goals of the context in which you work, and the goals of a particular preschool curriculum you may use. In particular, you can support preschool children as they work toward developing the following skills:

- Knowing and using people's names
- Initiating interactions
- Joining a group at work or play
- Making and taking suggestions
- Using words to express needs, rights, and feelings

- Maintaining relationships over time

- Taking turns

- Recognizing others' emotions and perspectives

- Negotiating conflicts in peaceful ways by compromising, bargaining, and standing up for their own and others' rights

- Showing awareness of and concern for others' rights, feelings, and well-being

- Demonstrating cooperation skills

- Demonstrating helping skills, such as sharing information or materials, giving physical assistance, and offering emotional support

- Recognizing and respecting people's similarities and differences

- Identifying emotions

- Acquiring and using language to express their emotions

- Understanding how circumstances and events influence personal emotions

- Understanding that they can affect how others feel and that people feel friendly toward those who are friendly toward them

- Increasing their understanding of fair and unfair, right and wrong, kind and unkind behaviors

- Demonstrating empathy for others

- Demonstrating care and respect for classroom materials

- Developing comfortable relationships beyond the family

- Communicating a belief in future potential for themselves

Facilitating Social-Emotional Development through Different Types of Play

In the following sections, you will find several illustrations of social and emotional competencies being supported in different areas of the preschool classroom, as well as outdoors. Note that some of these scenarios involve free play with limited teacher involvement and some involve guided play in which the teacher has initiated the play with particular purposes in mind. Both free and guided play are helpful for supporting children's social and emotional development.

Math and Manipulatives Center

In the following example, the teacher is planning for guided play and games with rules. She is particularly focused on the development of social skills for a child who is a dual language learner.

Turn Taking with Board Games

Mrs. Jones expects that all four children in the group will benefit from the opportunities to count up to ten and to practice one-to-one correspondence. One of the children Mrs. Jones has invited to the table is Rodrigo, a dual language learner who speaks Spanish well and has limited English language proficiency. Mrs. Jones plans to use the Hi Ho Cherry-O game to give Rodrigo practice with turn taking, with which he has some difficulty. This game is especially useful for this purpose, because Rodrigo knows the numbers from one to ten in both English and Spanish, so the math-language demands of this game are not difficult for him. He will therefore be able to focus more of his energy and attention on taking turns.

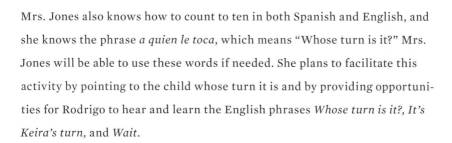

Mrs. Jones also knows how to count to ten in both Spanish and English, and she knows the phrase *a quien le toca*, which means "Whose turn is it?" Mrs. Jones will be able to use these words if needed. She plans to facilitate this activity by pointing to the child whose turn it is and by providing opportunities for Rodrigo to hear and learn the English phrases *Whose turn is it?*, *It's Keira's turn,* and *Wait.*

With greater turn-taking experience, as well as the English language skills to support turn taking, Rodrigo will become better equipped to understand the turn-taking process and turn-taking words in less clear-cut, more complicated, and challenging situations.

Block Center

Miss Appleton is particularly focused on supporting Ronnie, who has autism spectrum disorder (ASD), in developing social skills. Children with ASD often have difficulty with language, communication, and social relationships. Social play can be especially difficult but is an important step toward socialization and learning for all children. Right now, Miss Appleton is working toward helping Ronnie accept playing in the same space as another child. This is a small but significant step in the direction of playing with others and sharing the same materials.

Learning to Share Space

Miss Appleton has selected the floor-toys area because Ronnie plays here frequently and is comfortable in this area. She equips the center with a variety of toys with which Ronnie enjoys playing and allows him to play there alone as he chooses for a day or two. Meanwhile, Miss Appleton identifies a patient, socially skilled, accepting peer buddy who would likely be willing to play in the floor toys center with Ronnie. She invites that child, Kara, to serve as Ronnie's play buddy. When Kara agrees, Miss Appleton explains that she will be helping Ronnie learn how to play and that Miss Appleton will tell her what to do.

For the first days, Miss Appleton tells Kara how to play beside Ronnie for just a few minutes without interacting. The length of these side-by-side play episodes is increased by a couple of minutes each day until it is clear that Ronnie is accepting of playing in the same space with Kara. Only then does Ms. Appleton encourage Ronnie and Kara to play together with the same materials and eventually to interact.

Art Center

In the following illustration, we see an example of free creative play. The teacher briefly steps into the children's play to help them further develop their emotional competence.

OBSERVE AND LEARN:
Using Language to Express Emotions

At the end of morning circle and before dismissing children to begin free-choice time, Ms. Jenny reminds them of some of the options that are available to them. As she points out the double side-by-side easel, Ms. Jenny suggests that one way children might choose to paint at the easel today could be to paint the way they feel.

Ten minutes after free-choice time begins, Ms. Jenny notices Shanteria and Olivia painting side by side. Shanteria is painting in dark shades of brown, black, and grey, while Olivia is using a lot of red and orange. Ms. Jenny says, "I see you both using different colors. I'm wondering about your paintings. I'd like to hear about them." Shanteria says, "I'm painting about my Grandma Owens."

Ms. Jenny says with interest, "Tell me about Grandma Owens in that painting."

"I love my grandma," Shanteria responds. "She is brown with black and grey hair."

Ms. Jenny replies, "Oh, I see. How do you feel when you are painting that picture?" Shanteria says, "Happy!" and then adds, "cuddly and warm and soft."

Ms. Jenny says, "Happy! It sounds like you also feel comfortable and relaxed when you are with Grandma Owens." Shanteria smiles and nods in agreement.

Olivia, who has been listening, says, "I am painting 'my brother broke my pinwheel.'" Ms. Jenny asks, "He broke it?"

Olivia exclaims, "I'm painting mad."

Ms. Jenny says, "You do sound mad. In fact, you sound furious! That is really mad." "That's why it is all red. I'm furious," says Olivia.

Playground

This is an example of rough-and-tumble play. The teacher mostly remains outside of the play as children have opportunities to develop their emotional competence.

Roger, Alton, and Ayla often engage in a game of chasing and catching while on the playground. They appear to enjoy the activity and to be motivated to continue this play from one day to the next. As a result of this ongoing experience, they are learning to read one another's emotional signals. Although the physical activity is intense, they recognize cues in body posture and facial expression that indicate that the game is "just pretend."  On the rare occasions when one of the children becomes genuinely angry or distressed, the others are able to see it in the set of the upset child's eyes and mouth. They have learned to back off from the act of catching when the signals tell them, "I'm upset for real."

The teacher keeps an eye on their play and has occasionally pointed out instances to these children in which someone appears to be genuinely distressed. This need has become rarer as these children have learned to read emotional cues. With a few other children, the teacher has found the need to directly teach a verbal signal, "Stop. I want a break," with a hand firmly raised to signal *stop*.

The teacher in this example recognizes the important ways that rough-and-tumble play contributes to children's emotional and physical competence, as well as their self-regulation. She uses strategies to enable and manage this play so that children are not hurt.

Creating Play Plans to Support Social and Emotional Development

This section presents a framework you can use as you make your own plans to support social-emotional goals through play. The first example is a possible play plan that could be used to support the goal that children will show confidence in a range of abilities, as well as in the capacity to accomplish tasks and take on new tasks. The second example is a possible play plan to support the goals that children will negotiate conflicts in peaceful ways by compromising, bargaining, and standing up for their own and others' rights and will complete an activity or project in conjunction with another child or small group.

Use these examples to develop your own play plans to support social-emotional goals that you identify as important for the children you teach. You might draw these goals from the list provided in this chapter, from your state's early learning standards, and from the preschool curriculum you use. In addition, consider the following reflection questions to use after you develop and implement your play plans, to evaluate the usefulness of those plans:

- How did the children respond to the provocations I provided? What did they do or say?

- What support strategies did I use? How did the children respond to my support strategies? What did they do or say?

- What evidence did I see or hear that children were moving in the direction of my identified goals?

- What might I do differently, if I were to implement this or a similar plan again?

- What will my next step be, with regard to helping the children move toward the goals?

Free-Play Plan

Before the Play: Acting as Planner

Let's imagine that you have noticed recently that a couple of the children in your class often build towers using the large unit blocks, which are the only blocks currently available in the block center. As they do this, they seem to challenge themselves to build the towers as tall as they can. You have noticed that they seem to experience pride in their tower-building accomplishments. You decide that the time is ripe to capitalize upon this interest that these children have displayed.

Goals
You think about important learning and development goals that block play supports. One of these, which is especially evident in your observations of these young children, is that they show confidence in their abilities and their capacity to accomplish tasks.

Setting and Time
You decide to continue to encourage this activity in the block center during free-play time.

Preparation and Materials
Because the children have progressively grown in their ability to stack the unit blocks as high as they can go, you decide to create some challenge by adding smaller blocks

to the block center. You place a large number of 2" x 2" cube blocks in a big basket on the floor of the block center.

Provocations

For now, you decide to allow the newly added blocks to serve as the sole provocation for the children's play. You decide to just watch and see what the children do with the blocks on the first morning that they are placed in the block center.

Recall that *scaffolding* involves providing only as much support as a child needs to be successful. In this case, simply providing the new smaller blocks may be enough for your goal of supporting the children's confidence in their accomplishments. As the children strive to out-do their previous performances, you may decide to provide additional encouragement and support.

During the Play: Acting as Guide

As you think ahead to what might occur now that the small blocks are added, you consider the following support strategies:

- If the children do not think of creating towers with the smaller blocks, you could spend a moment in parallel play at the block center and begin to create a small block tower of your own. The children may simply notice what you have done, or you could draw attention to it verbally: "Oh look, these blocks can be made into towers, too."

- If the children do not come up with it on their own, prompt them to place the first cube block on a solid foundation such as a large unit block, since the low pile of the carpet in your block center might make it harder to balance these small blocks. You could say, "Hmm, the carpet makes that a little wobbly. How about putting this big rectangular block as the base?" or "Can you think of some way to make the small blocks more stable? Maybe some sort of a sturdy base?"

- You could demonstrate your interest in the children's activity and accomplishments by comments such as, "You're balancing those blocks slowly and carefully," or "I think that one was taller than the last tower you made."

After the Play: Promoting Reflection

Documentation

You take a photograph of one of the towers that the two children created together.

Reflection and Representation

Showing the photo to them after play, you encourage the children to reflect on their experience. You ask the children, "Was it harder or easier building with the smaller blocks?" and "What did you have to do to build such a tall tower?" You suggest, "If you build towers this afternoon, you might decide that you want to draw a picture of how many blocks you use."

Use the reflection questions provided on page 55 to aid you in evaluating your play plan.

Guided-Play Plan

Before the Play: Acting as Planner

Let's imagine that you have recently started a thematic unit titled "Animals at the Zoo." You anticipate that this unit will continue for two or three weeks, as the children have shown a lot of interest. You have read several books to them about zoos and the animals found there and have shown them a short informational video. You have noticed that a small group of the children are spending a lot of playground time pretending to be animals in a zoo and pulling together playground equipment—buckets, a trike, a wagon—in an effort to create enclosures. Some conflicts have arisen due to a limited supply of materials for creating the large-scale representation of a zoo that the children seem to have in mind. You decide to provide an indoor opportunity for the children to work together to create a miniature zoo.

Goals

You see this activity as a great opportunity to support children's social skills, as well as to help them learn more information about the theme of the unit. You recognize that this activity can be used to help children learn to negotiate conflicts in peaceful ways by compromising, bargaining, and standing up for their own and others' rights and to complete a project in conjunction with another child or small group.

Setting and Time

You decide that center time will be the best time for this activity. In your classroom, center time lasts for an hour and is based on a twenty-minute rotation system. You anticipate that the zoo construction will not be completed in a single center rotation, so you plan for the activity to continue into afternoon center time and possibly over a couple of days.

Preparation and Materials

Since the project will not be completed in one session, you decide to provide a two-foot square piece of thin plywood for the children to work on. You provide a large block of modeling dough, small sticks, leaves and stones from outdoors, pipe cleaners, small boxes, wooden craft sticks, and a set of small plastic animals.

Provocations

You have already provided provocations in the form of the books and videos and the several days of thematic content that have been part of the "Animals at the Zoo" unit. You mention to the children that you've noticed they have been playing zoo outside, and you now have some materials they can use to create a miniature zoo inside. Explain that they will not each have their own materials to make their own zoo. The challenge is to create one zoo, using the materials together.

During the Play: Acting as Guide

Consider the following possible support strategies:

- One of your roles will be to observe and listen to the children's progress and to offer support as needed.

- Look for opportunities to describe what the children are doing, especially in relation to the social goals you have identified. For example, "I heard that you asked Robbie to explain his idea," or "I notice Philip and Marta sharing the modeling dough to make a lot of caves."

If children experience a conflict of ideas, you can assist them in negotiating the conflict with a question. For example, if one child wants to create cages and another wants the animals to have more natural enclosures, you might ask, "Can you find a *compromise*—a solution that would be okay with both of you?" Or you might make a suggestion, such as, "Maybe some of the animals can be in cages and some in other enclosures," or provide a reminder, such as, "Liam, listen to Marta's idea."

The best support is not too little, not too much, but just enough. If children experience a disagreement, you could start out with the lowest level of support you think might be helpful, such as, "Remember to use your words to figure this out." If that is not enough, you may have to provide more structure, such as, "Liam, tell Marta what you think the problem is. Then Marta will tell you what she thinks the problem is."

After the Play: Promoting Reflection

Documentation
Jot down notes about instances of children working cooperatively and resolving differences of opinion. Read these to the children later in the day.

Reflection and Representation
Later at snack time, encourage the children to talk about one thing that was fun about working on the zoo and one thing that was difficult.

Use the reflection questions provided on page 55 to aid you in evaluating your play plan.

Create Your Own Play Plan

Use the template provided below. Start with one or two social-emotional goals; you could use the list provided in this chapter, your state's early learning standards, or the curriculum you use. Then, based on your knowledge of the children you teach and their interests, abilities, and the kinds of things they like to play, think about a play plan that helps children move toward the goals. You can refer to chapter 2 if you want a reminder about the many different types of play that you may provide for and encourage. You can refer to chapter 3 to review the possible support roles and strategies you may use to support children's play and reach the goals you identified.

Before the Play

Goals

_____

_____

Setting and Time

_____

_____

Preparation and Materials

_____

_____

Provocations

_____

_____

_____

During the Play

Possible Support Strategies

_____

_____

_____

After the Play

Documentation

_____

_____

_____

Reflection and Representation

_____

_____

_____

five

5

Developing Self-Regulation

The preschool years are a critically important time during which children are developing the ability to be self-regulated. Self-regulation consists of a complex set of skills. Often considered an aspect of social-emotional competence, the topic of self-regulation is central to preschoolers' optimal development and school readiness. As children grow from toddlerhood through the preschool years into the early years of elementary school, they are developing their abilities to regulate their physical behaviors, emotional behaviors, and aspects of their thinking. Many aspects of self-regulation are often thought of as areas of cognitive development. This is another example of the importance of taking the whole-child view of learning and development.

A person who is self-regulated is able to manage himself rather than rely on external regulation. Of course, this process of development is gradual and takes a long time. As the preschoolers in your care are growing in self-regulation, they are developing the ability to do such things as delay gratification, control impulses, pay intentional attention, resist temptation, and make and carry out plans. These are all characteristics that teachers of preschoolers can appreciate.

Self-Regulation as a Foundation for Learning

If children never developed self-regulation, they would remain dependent on others to regulate their behavior for them. If a child were entirely dependent on external regulation by an adult, he might be able to sustain appropriate behavior, at least for a while, when the adult is present, but he would not be able to control himself in the adult's absence.

Self-regulation is a central component of school readiness. The ability to self-regulate underlies all kinds of learning. A growing research base shows that the abilities that comprise self-regulation are stronger predictors of children's school readiness and achievement than IQ or family background. Research also shows that kindergarten teachers rate aspects of self-regulation, such as impulse control and the ability to follow directions, as being more important to children's kindergarten readiness than academic skills such as letter recognition. Children with good self-regulation skills are better able to get along with their peers and teachers, engage in fewer problem behaviors, and experience fewer conflicts. Children with healthy self-regulation abilities are also more able to persist in challenging learning tasks. It is easy to understand the importance of self-regulation to children's success in school and in life in general.

You may be surprised to learn just how central play is to the development of young children's self-regulation. We often think of play as a very free and spontaneous activity, and it often is. However, some structural characteristics built into children's play are not so obvious until you take a closer look. Recent research shows that games with rules and sociodramatic play are virtually indispensable to the development of self-regulation in early childhood.

Sociodramatic Play and Self-Regulation

First, let's look at sociodramatic play, which we have already defined as a type of pre-tend play in which two or more children interact with a shared goal. This kind of play is a leading activity during the preschool and kindergarten years because it is so crucial to the development of self-regulation. When children engage in mature sociodramatic play, they take on roles. For example, one child may be the doctor and the other may be a baby patient. The roles have rules: Babies do not take doctors' temperatures, and doctors do not drink from a baby bottle. Babies do not say, "I'd prefer a shot in the arm."

They just say, "Waaaaa!" In mature sociodramatic play, children stick to the requirements of their roles, at least until they decide to adopt a new role and announce it. Children talk about what is going to happen in the play before they do it. Because children generally enjoy the process of sociodramatic play, they are motivated to self-regulate their behavior during this kind of play, to stick to the restrictions implicit in the play, and to inhibit impulses to do something that is not in accord with the rules. They are motivated to do what is required by the play, to keep the play going. Research has shown that preschool children are better able to self-regulate in the context of social pretend play than in the real world, and the self-regulation practice that children gain through pretend play contributes to their ability to be self-regulated outside of play. In fact, in studies in which adults have taught preschoolers to engage in more mature sociodramatic play, the children showed significant growth in their self-regulation behaviors both within and outside of play.

Games with Rules and Self-Regulation

Games with rules become popular with children in the later preschool years and the early years of elementary school. Remember that playing games with rules involves a competition between individuals or teams, and it is regulated by either longstanding rules or rules by temporary agreement. Games with rules for preschoolers may include simple board games such as Chutes and Ladders, Candy Land, Hi Ho Cherry-O, checkers, picture dominos, and bingo. They can also include large motor games such as Freeze Tag, Simon Says, Mother May I, Duck-Duck-Goose, and relay races.

The link between games with rules and self-regulation is perhaps more immediately obvious than the link between sociodramatic play and self-regulation. In games with rules, the rules are explicit. To play the game, children must be taught the rules of procedure, either by an adult or a more knowledgeable child. This takes time, effort, and concentration. Learning to monitor their own actions in comparison to a clear standard of behavior—the rule—is important preparation for children's later learning in the elementary school years.

By definition, games with rules are competitive; someone will win and someone will lose. Learning to lose in the context of a game helps prepare children for the frustrations and temporary failures that they will encounter in later learning. One of the benefits of games with rules is that the child can have opportunities to play again, which can help to build persistence and the ability to delay gratification. Even though the child didn't win this time, he might win later. By the way, it is important to mention that the competitive nature of games with rules does not imply that noncompetitive, cooperative games are not also valuable. Many prosocial skills can be practiced through cooperative games. The point here is that competitive games have some special advantages in helping children to develop the skills of self-regulation.

Providing Guidance for Learning Self-Regulation

Preschool teachers are in an excellent position to support the development of self-regulation skills. Outside of play, you can support children's growing self-regulation by providing a developmentally appropriate curriculum, communicating clear expectations and rules, and using guidance and discipline strategies designed to gradually move children toward being able to manage themselves.

As a tool and context for promoting self-regulation, play is best used by teachers intentionally and knowledgeably. Many children come to preschool without the expected levels of self-regulation ability. In fact, some research even suggests that the seven-year-olds of today display, in general, self-regulation abilities similar to those of the five-year-olds of the 1940s. In addition, many children today come to preschool with very little experience in the kind of mature sociodramatic play that contributes to the development of self-regulation. As a preschool teacher, your role in this process includes making provisions for play—time, space, and materials—as well as scaffolding children's ability to engage in the kind of mature play that can increase their self-regulation. Be prepared to do more than simply set the stage for this kind of play; inexperienced children need play guidance.

Although play outside of school can give children ways to learn and exercise these types of skills, the opportunities for play in communities and families can vary greatly. As Elena Bodrova and Deborah Leong note in *Tools of the Mind*, "Play used to be something that children learned at home; they then brought these play skills to the classroom. Children used to play in neighborhoods in mixed-age groups that included children from three to ten years of age and even older. It is a very sad fact that children do not play the way they used to." If children aren't learning self-regulation through neighborhood play, then exercising these skills at school becomes even more beneficial.

So, what does that play guidance look like? Chapter 3 provided several examples of your potential roles in planning for, guiding, and following up on children's play. Mature sociodramatic play allows children to adopt roles, play according to the rules of their roles, create pretend scenarios together, and talk about the scenarios and their roles. The list that follows provides some examples from preschool and kindergarten. In line with guidance on developmentally appropriate practice from NAEYC and researchers Bodrova and Leong, children engaged in high-quality sociodramatic play tend to do the following:

- Create and act out pretend scenarios

- Invent props to fit their roles

- Play rich and multifaceted roles that have specific characteristics or rules for action

- Engage in long dialogues about the whats, whos, and hows of the scenario

- Coordinate multiple roles and themes

- Engage in extended discussions about roles, actions, and props

- Solve disputes and disagreements

- Become immersed in play so that it can continue the next day or for several days

Before the Play: Acting as Planner

Before the play begins, there are strategies you can use to increase the likelihood that mature sociodramatic play will emerge.

- **Provide simple dress-up items to help children designate their roles.** It is not necessary to provide full-blown costumes for specific roles; children can use their creativity and imagination to mentally transform, for example, a silky scarf into long hair, a cape, or a tail.

- **Provide props that include both realistic and more flexible items.** For those children who are just developing their pretending skills, using more realistic items such as a small teapot can help them to remember the scenario of the play and can reduce the need for a lot of communication concerning the pot's identity and purpose. On the other hand, more flexible props, such as a small block of Styrofoam, can exercise and challenge children's imaginative and communication abilities as they transform the item into a cell phone or a shaving razor to support their roles and actions.

- **Provide provocations, such as a book, a thematic unit, or a field trip.** For example, imagine that you have set up the dramatic play center with props and costumes suggestive of a bakery. You can provoke children's play ideas by reading a book about bakeries and then intentionally pointing out to children the various bakery-related roles and actions shown in the book, as well as things that people may say to one another in a bakery. You can take the provocation one step further and suggest to the children that these are people they may want to pretend to be and actions they may want to pretend to do.

- **Provide reminders.** On the walls of the dramatic play center, you can post photos of various roles and sequences of action—such as images of a baker, a cashier, or a cake decorator and actions of rolling out dough, running a cash register, or creating cake designs—that children may choose to engage in based on the current props provided. With these prompts as support, children may choose to enact them or build from them as they construct new ideas.

- **Incorporate a brief planning time at the beginning of play.** To help children think about their play intentions, make choices, and plan, huddle with those children who have selected to begin in the dramatic play center, and listen to their ideas about what they may want to play about and what they want to do and be. Encourage them to listen to one another and to work out conflicting ideas.

- **Provide sufficient time for play.** For young children to become immersed in complex, high-level sociodramatic play—the kind that supports the development of self-regulation—a block of time of forty to sixty minutes tends to work well.

During the Play: Acting as Guide

Consider which strategies you can use to enhance the level of children's sociodramatic play or to help prevent high-level play from falling apart. One of your most important roles is that of an observer. By monitoring the progress of children's play, you can assess what supports individual children may need, and you can make good decisions about providing the right level of support. When you observe, you may also be serving as a supportive presence. Sometimes just knowing that an adult is attentive and available can help children to relax into the play and bring forth their best effort.

Suggesting ideas is one way of supporting play. You can make verbal suggestions, such as, "You might want another customer in your store," to help when children have difficulty incorporating a new role into their scenario. You can make indirect suggestions in the form of adding props to the play situation: "Here are some pieces of fabric I found. Maybe you can find a way to use them in your campsite." Describing what you see is another way to give hints. For example, saying, "I see a lot of cakes being made. I'm trying to think what else they make in bakeries," might encourage children to come up with new ideas in play. A simple comment might be all that is needed to prompt more elaborate thinking.

You can encourage more mature players to provide support for less mature players. For example, "Susi, can you help Malia think of some ideas for what she could do here in the circus? Help her figure out different people she could choose to be."

Another way of coaching children in sociodramatic play is to refer them to the pictorial reminders you have placed on the wall. "Let's take a look at these pictures of what people do in a hair salon."

Occasionally you may want to briefly enter the children's play to model a solution or a new behavior. "A lot of clean dishes are piling up in the restaurant kitchen. I'll be the kitchen worker who puts them back in the cabinet," or "Since the queen won't let us go to the ball, I think I'll find something to do in the enchanted forest."

Keep in mind that as the adult, you shouldn't take over or direct children's sociodramatic play. If you do, it is no longer play and loses much of its benefit. Furthermore, if you become too involved in the play, your ability to watch, analyze, and provide appropriate support is compromised. As with other kinds of support, if you do become involved in the play itself, it is important to gradually withdraw the support of your involvement as soon as it is feasible, so children can remain in charge of the play.

After the Play: Promoting Reflection

After the play, there are strategies you can use to get the most out of the play that has occurred, as well as to enhance the chances that the play episode will be extended into later parts of the day or to the next day.

Immediately after the play period, you can remind children of the plans they had for play and then ask them to describe what they actually did. Always remember that the point is not to evaluate whether or not children actually did what they intended but to make them aware of themselves as decision makers. Further, ask the children what they enjoyed about the play and what they did not, and how they may want to carry the play episode into the future.

Referring to the pictorial postings of possible roles and actions to play, you might ask children, "Did you do any of the things pictured on the poster? What did you do?" or if not, "What did you do instead?" Encourage them to think about extending the play in the future: "What do you think you might decide to do next time you play in the dramatic play center (or bakery or grocery store)?"

Identifying Goals for Self-Regulation

For children to master self-regulation, they need to develop the following skills:

- Control impulses
- Resist temptation
- Delay gratification
- Enact positive behaviors
- Resist peer pressure
- Monitor own behavior
- Make choices and decisions
- Develop plans
- Persist at tasks
- Pay intentional attention
- Focus and concentrate
- Become aware of own thought process
- Follow simple rules, routines, and directions
- Shift attention between tasks
- Move through transitions

These skills contribute to children's growing ability to gradually manage themselves as they slowly become less dependent on others to provide external structure and regulation.

Facilitating Self-Regulation through Different Types of Play

Although play is not the only process through which young children develop self-regulation, it is a very important one. In the following example, we see sociodramatic play in which the teacher helps children to make decisions and plans and to adhere to their roles.

Playing Supermarket

In Mr. Kantowski's class, the children are involved in the second week of a thematic unit on the topic of food. The dramatic play center is set up for supermarket play. There is a collection of clean, empty food cans with the labels still attached, empty food boxes and containers, and a variety of other empty bottles and boxes. There is a cash register, pretend money, and grocery bags, along with purses, wallets, and two doll strollers that can be used as grocery carts.

At the end of circle time, which occurs immediately prior to free-choice time, Mr. Kantowski reminds children of the various centers available in the classroom. He also reminds them of a few of the play options available within those centers. When he describes the supermarket center, he quickly reminds the children of the materials there and asks the children to recall some of the roles that can be played in the grocery center: shopper, shopper's child, cashier, bagger, stocker, bakery worker, and deli worker.

Once each child has chosen his beginning center, Mr. Kantowski waits about five minutes to allow the children to initiate and organize their activities. He goes first to the supermarket center to check into how the play is progressing. Five children are in this center. He observes for a moment, and then asks of no one in particular, "What is happening here today?"

Children respond, "Shopping," and "I'm selling food," and "I'm getting tomatoes for dinner."

Mr. Kantowksi then asks each child, "Who are you today?" Each describes his role except Janelle, who simply shrugs. Mr. Kantowski says, "Hmmm . . . I wonder who Janelle can be." Jason suggests that she could be a person who is looking for cat food, and Janelle agrees with an enthusiastic nod of her head. Mr. Kantowski suggests that Janelle might need help to know where the cat food is and which kind to buy. Jason eagerly jumps in with advice to Janelle.

In this example, Mr. Kantowski helps children make choices, decisions, and plans through implementing a quick planning time and then following through as the play progresses. Mr. Kantowski's role in helping children to resist impulses is less obvious and less direct. He has provided the opportunity and motivation for children to stick with a play role—for a period of time, at least—by providing an interesting setting for make-believe play embedded within a thematic unit designed to build children's awareness of content to play about. While he could remind children of the roles they have chosen as the play progresses, he may want to do this in an indirect way that encourages children to reflect on the relationship between their role choices and the continuation of the play; for example, "Jason, if you switch from being a cashier to being a baby, who will take the customers' money?" This might lead to posting a Help Wanted sign to recruit a new cashier. On the other hand, Mr. Kantowski might want to leave it to the children to figure out the solution to the problem created when the cashier becomes a baby.

Play can support understanding of rules and why rules are important. In the following example, the teacher helps children learn the rules of a game and begin to understand how the rules help make the game fun. The children have opportunities to learn to delay gratification, resist temptation, and follow simple rules.

OBSERVE AND LEARN:
Table Games

In Miss Kelly's classroom, one of the centers is referred to as the table games center. This center has a variety of simple games available on a rotating basis. This week Miss Kelly is adding picture dominos, which has not been present in the center for a long time.

Each domino-like card is divided in half, with a picture on each side of the dividing line. Because this game is no longer familiar to the children, Miss Kelly takes several minutes at the end of circle time to remind children of the rules of picture dominos: Turn all of the cards facedown. Each child selects seven cards, which they place on their racks and keep secret from the other players. The first player places a domino card faceup in the center of the table. Let's say the card has a cat on one side of the line and an apple on the other side. The next player looks at his dominos to see if he has one with either cat or an apple. If he does, he places the card so that the picture touches its match. If the player does not have a match, he discards one domino and selects another from the pile and places it on his rack.

Miss Kelly uses an "I do, we do, you do" process to teach the rules of the game. First, she demonstrates as if she were the first player; she conducts a couple of rounds of the game with a selected child volunteer as her opponent. Then, she selects another child volunteer to take over her own role, so that two children are demonstrating the game to the group. After children have seen this demonstration and as they participate in the game at the table games center, Miss Kelly uses this strategy as children need reminders about the rules of the game.

Once children have learned how to play the game independently, they experience opportunities to cheat or to abandon the game. The fun of the play itself serves as motivation to delay gratification and to resist the temptation to cheat by peeking. The reaction of the playmate: "Hey! No cheating!" or Miss Kelly's interventions: "It is more fun if you don't peek," may serve as further motivation to resist temptation, delay gratification, and follow the rules.

Creating Play Plans to Support Development of Self-Regulation

Free-Play Plan

Before the Play: Acting as Planner

Let's imagine that two of the children in your class have recently been camping with their families. This has resulted in spontaneous camp-themed play. On the playground, you notice that these two children have interested a few others in their play. The small group is using the outdoor playhouse as their tent and has gathered sticks and twigs to build a campfire. The play has continued for two days, and the group seems to be quite enthused about their activity.

Goals

You decide that you want to intentionally capitalize upon children's motivation to engage in pretend play within this newfound interest. Knowing that mature sociodramatic play is an activity which ultimately aids children's abilities to monitor their own behavior and control impulses, you intend to support them in their engagement.

Looking back to the characteristics of mature sociodramatic play, you can keep these in mind as behaviors you may support. For example, you might identify "invent props to fit their roles," "coordinate multiple roles and themes," or "become immersed in play so that it can continue the next day or for several days."

Setting and Time

Because the outdoor environment during playground time is the setting in which these children are currently engaging in this play, you decide to encourage the continuation of play in that context.

Preparation and Materials

To support possible new directions in which the children may take their camping play, you decide to add a few simple props, including both realistic and more abstract items that can be transformed in a variety of ways. From some of the children's parents, you borrow several old flashlights that no longer work, a lantern, a couple of small backpacks, a few campfire cooking pots, and some old blankets. In anticipation that this may lead to more children being interested in camping play, you also plan to use ropes and a couple of the old blankets to create simple tents. You could string ropes between trees and toss the blankets over the ropes or drape a blanket over a picnic table.

Provocations

One of your colleagues suggests a children's book called *Bailey Goes Camping* by Kevin Henkes, which describes several typical camping activities. These descriptions are embedded within an engaging story about a child who plays camping at home because he is too young to go along on his siblings' scout camping trip. You decide the book is a great introduction to the basic possibilities inherent in a camping theme, and you plan to read it to the whole group at story time.

During the Play: Acting as Guide

Keeping in mind that your overarching purpose is to support children's engagement in mature sociodramatic play and the development of self-regulation abilities, you provide a variety of support strategies. By giving a little thought to these beforehand, you are primed to notice when opportunities arise to use them.

- **Paraphrase:** When children become involved in a dispute about how the scenario should progress, you paraphrase their perspectives to one another: "Jonathan, Sam is saying you could search for firewood together. Tell him your idea."

- **Question:** One child becomes disgruntled when another plugs an imaginary TV into a tree, as it does not match with his image of camping possibilities. You ask, "Sahar, do you think people ever bring a TV camping? How could they do that?"

- **Model:** The children seem to be running out of ideas after cooking their supper over the campfire, so you briefly step in and model marshmallow roasting or a sing-around-the-campfire activity. As children either take over on their own or decide they don't want to do what you have modeled, you step out of the activity.

In a free-play scenario that has arisen from the children's own interests and initiative, the need for your involvement may be minimal. Remember that your purpose is to provide opportunity for the growth of self-regulation by encouraging and supporting mature sociodramatic play only to the degree that your help is needed. By monitoring the situation and keeping your goals and potential roles in mind, you can make informed decisions about what kind of scaffolding to provide.

After the Play: Promoting Reflection

Documentation
Take photographs of children's play activity, and show these at snack time as prompts to encourage children to discuss new directions for the play and/or ways to combine the theme with other popular playground activities. Children may decide, for example, that tomorrow they will "hike into town" (walk to the sandbox) to purchase the sandwiches being made there.

Reflection and Representation
You can encourage children to create a class book about camping. Each child who wants to can create a picture illustrating some aspect of camping. When the picture is complete, the child can dictate a line or two for you to write on a facing page. Laminate and bind the individual pages together with string or metal loops, and you have a book that children can use to revisit their camping play experiences. You can place the book where children can access it in one of the book-reading areas of your classroom.

Guided-Play Plan

Before the Play: Acting as Planner

Let's imagine you are teaching a group of younger preschoolers, ages two-and-a-half to three years. At this age, many children are still working on the basic physical aspects of self-regulation. You decide to introduce a fun game to give the children practice with stopping and starting. You select the game of Freeze Dance, which involves dancing while the music is playing and then stopping movement by "freezing" when the music stops.

Goals
Through this game, the children will have opportunities to monitor their own behavior; pay intentional attention; control impulses; and follow simple rules, routines, and directions.

Setting and Time
After considering the possibilities, you decide to teach this game during a brief on-the-rug time that is scheduled between playground time and lunch. You choose this time in part because it can serve as a bridge between the high activity of playground time and the quieter activity of lunch. After playing the Freeze Dance game, you plan to sing a quiet song with the children and then dismiss them gradually to wash their hands and go to the lunch tables.

Preparation and Materials
To teach the basic Freeze Dance game, you use a recording of one of the children's favorite songs.

Provocations
You might choose to introduce the game with a simple challenge, such as, "In this game, you get to show me how you can control your body and make it stop moving—make it 'freeze.' Controlling your body is an important part of growing up."

During the Play: Acting as Guide

You could initially teach this game using an "I do, we do, you do" strategy. First, the children sit and watch as you dance and freeze according to the song. Next, invite the children to stand up and do it with you. Finally, you sit down and watch as the children do it.

As the children are learning the game, you can provide encouragement in the form of descriptive statements, such as, "Aisha froze very still!" "Sasha, you were able to stop yourself that time!" "I can tell you are listening very carefully for the 'freeze' signal," and, "Sometimes it can be hard to stop. Keep trying."

For a child who shows difficulty responding to the "freeze" signal, you could add support in the form of an additional cue that comes before freeze, perhaps tapping him on the shoulder to alert him that the signal is coming up.

Children with disabilities that affect their mobility can participate in this activity as well. For example, you might have a child in your classroom who uses a wheelchair or a child who needs positioning with supportive bolsters to sit on the floor. In addition to encouraging them to participate from their seated position, you could also engage the whole class in a seated version of the freeze game, in which everyone moves only their upper body.

As children become skilled with this game, you can add challenge by putting the original recording aside and using some other music of which you control the stopping and starting. Calling out, "Freeze," as you stop the music makes the game easier. Simply stopping the music is more challenging. Stopping at irregular intervals adds challenge as well. By gradually removing cues and supports, you are adding challenge to the activity.

After the Play: Promoting Reflection

Documentation
You may want to make notes to yourself regarding which children have a lot of trouble stopping themselves. Create some easier opportunities for them to practice this skill, perhaps with music that has a slower tempo.

Reflection and Representation
You could ask children to think about whether they've learned any tricks for stopping themselves, and encourage them to try to describe these.

Ask yourself the following reflection questions:

- How did the children respond to the provocations I provided? What did they do and/or say?

- What support strategies did I use? How did the children respond to my support strategies? What did they do and/or say?

- What evidence did I see or hear that children were moving in the direction of my identified goals?

- What might I do differently if I were to implement this or a similar plan again?

- What will my next step be, with regard to helping the children move toward this goal?

Create Your Own Play Plan

Use the template provided below. Start with one or two self-regulation goals. You could identify them from the list provided in this chapter, from your state's early learning standards, or from the curriculum you use. Then, based on your knowledge of the children you teach—their interests, their abilities, and the kinds of things they like to play—think about how to create a play plan that helps children move toward the goals. Refer to chapter 2 to remind yourself of the many different types of play that you may provide for and encourage. Refer to chapter 3 to remind yourself about possible support roles and strategies you may use to support children's play with regard to the goals you identified.

Before the Play

Goals

_____

_____

Setting and Time

_____

_____

Preparation and Materials

_____

_____

Provocations

_____

_____

During the Play

Possible Support Strategies

_____

_____

After the Play

Documentation

_____

_____

Reflection and Representation

_____

_____

six

6

Promoting Mathematical Learning

Some may think preschoolers are too young for mathematical learning, wondering, "Shouldn't we wait until children are older before introducing them to math?" In truth, we do not need to introduce young children to mathematics; they have already met! Children are surrounded by mathematics. Math is an integral part of our world. It is everywhere we turn. An infant sees the edge of his blanket with its border decorated with a pattern of embroidered images: puppy, duck, ball, puppy, duck, ball, puppy, duck, ball. Every day as he lies upon and cuddles his blanket, he is exposed to this repeated pattern. Pattern recognition is a mathematics fundamental underlying algebraic understanding, as well as supporting the development of number sense and spatial sense.

I recall my own son as a toddler in a room with toys and several of his beloved pacifiers scattered across the rug. Of his own initiative, he toddled around the room picking up pacifiers (and only pacifiers) and placing them in a pail. This capacity to distinguish the pacifiers from all of the other "not pacifiers" and collect them into a group is fundamental to the ability to sort and classify. While his knowledge was at a basic intuitive level, it was there.

Young children see numerals, patterns, and collections all around them. As they play with a group of balls, they notice that one is bigger than another, even before they have the words big and little in their vocabulary. They perceive that a bowl containing five M&M's has fewer candies than a bowl containing one hundred, before they have the words for more and fewer and before they can count.

Importance of Early Mathematical Learning

Consider the following:

- Preschool children show an interest in the everyday math that is naturally part of their world. In fact, a study of preschoolers engaged in free play by

Herbert Ginsburg and Kyoung-Hye Seo showed that during almost half of the fifteen-minute segments that were observed, children's natural play contained the roots of mathematical learning. Young children often choose to play with mathematical ideas.

- Much of mathematical learning is sequential. Until the basics are understood, it is difficult if not impossible to learn many of the more sophisticated concepts with true understanding.

- For a long time, international studies have shown that children in the United States trail those in other countries in terms of math achievement. A lack of solid understanding of mathematics can limit children in their everyday lives and in future work possibilities.

Young children are interested in mathematical learning. Later mathematical learning is built upon basic concepts that preschoolers can learn, and mathematical learning is important to children's future success in life. So supporting children's mathematical learning in the preschool years is vital.

Developing Mathematics Understanding through Play

In their joint position statement on early childhood mathematics, the National Council of Teachers of Mathematics (NCTM) and NAEYC recommend that we "provide ample time, materials, and teacher support for children to engage in play, a context in which they explore and manipulate mathematical ideas with keen interest." At the same time, these organizations make clear that, while free play provides important opportunities for mathematical learning, it is not enough by itself. Effective preschool programs also provide intentionally organized learning activities to coherently build children's understanding of mathematics over time. Effective mathematics education for preschoolers includes free play, guided play, and a carefully sequenced and developmentally appropriate math curriculum. A strong message of NCTM and NAEYC's position statement is the need to "go beyond sporadic, hit-or-miss mathematics. In effective programs, teachers make judicious use of a variety of approaches, strategies, and materials to support children's interest and ability in mathematics."

While a full mathematics curriculum is beyond the scope of this book, both free play and guided play contribute in important ways to children's mathematical learning in preschool. One important function of free play for math learning is that it offers children opportunities to practice and apply what they learn about math outside of free play. Free play also offers opportunities for children to "bump into" mathematical concepts in their play. Guided play can be used to increase the likelihood that children will encounter and engage with important mathematical concepts. In play, children encounter, explore, and make sense of their world—and their world is filled with math!

Intentional Teacher Support

Virtually all of the teacher roles described previously can be useful as you guide and support children's mathematical learning through play. Following are descriptions of a few roles that are especially important to mathematical play. Additional examples are provided through the scenarios and play plans in this chapter.

Before the Play: Acting as Planner

Awareness and understanding of the goals of early mathematics learning is very important. Understanding these goals is a basic foundation to planning and implementing any mathematical experience, including free-play and guided-play experiences. It is tempting to think that, as adults, we all know and understand the basic concepts of preschool mathematics. Even for those who do, some extra reading to refresh your knowledge is a good idea. Page 81 lists many central goals for early math learning and offers some helpful resources about early childhood math concepts. If you are intimidated by the mere mention of mathematics, then renewing your awareness of early math concepts will probably be quite reassuring to you. Basic math can be (and should be!) interesting and a lot of fun. Knowledge of early childhood mathematics will help you to identify the goals for a particular play activity and will help you to think ahead to possible provocations, materials, and supports to provide.

Many materials are available on the market to support children's mathematical play, and it is good to have some of these. A large set of unit blocks is essential. Most preschool classrooms are equipped with at least some unit blocks, and expanding that set is a worthy pursuit. Provide several sets of manipulatives that children can use for counting, sorting, and ordering. These can be purchased, made, or collected. Bottle caps in various sizes and or colors, small squares of sturdy paper, and cut segments of variously colored drinking straws from the dollar store are a few inexpensive possibilities.

Additional planning roles are described in the examples provided later in this chapter.

During the Play: Acting as Guide

Both free play and guided play are important, and neither one is enough on its own. Nowhere is this clearer than in mathematical play. While free play provides many opportunities for children to practice, apply, and discover important mathematical concepts, we cannot rely solely on the possibility that children will in fact do these things to their best benefit. Guided play is important to put mathematical learning possibilities right in a child's path so she will be exposed to those possibilities.

In guided play, you can initiate a play interaction with a child with a specific goal in mind, gently steer the interaction in the direction of the goal, and then be ready to support the child's learning as she picks up on the activity. Of course, the child may take the activity in a different direction than the goal you had intended. This is alright. If you continue to push your agenda, the activity is no longer play. You can try again later. And of course, you have chances to provide similar opportunities during more structured activities. Keep in mind that, while free play and guided play are extremely important contexts for preschoolers' learning and they should predominate, play is not the only beneficial activity that happens in a high-quality preschool environment.

One very important role for you during children's mathematical play is the role of providing vocabulary. Through this role, you are helping to "mathematize" a child's intuitive knowledge of math by providing words to use as they communicate and think about mathematical concepts. Words and phrases such as big, small, more than, less than, fewer than, the same, different, equal, square, circle, pattern, above, below, longer, shorter, set, and sequence are among the important vocabulary you can provide to children as they play. You can teach this language in context by using strategies such as modeling, paraphrasing, and describing.

Questioning is another valuable strategy for supporting children's mathematical learning during play. Use basic informational questions, such as, "Are there two triangles or three?" and "How many cars are there?" Also use more provocative questions, such as, "How do you know that there are more blue cars than red cars?" and "Tell Tara how you created these sets." In any play activity, take care not to overwhelm children with questions. One or two thoughtfully selected questions are often enough to enhance a child's thinking. Too many questions tend to interrupt the play, turn children off to the activity, and feel like a test.

When children are engaged in play of their own choosing, avoid the temptation to turn play that is not currently math related into a math lesson. For example, asking a child to count the blocks in her castle at a time when she is primarily interested in the fantasy scenario is not central to her play and is interruptive. This is an example of co-opting the child's play for your own purposes. On the other hand, if the child's play currently contains mathematical elements, such as when a child is placing blocks on the shelf according to the shape outlines that are attached to the shelf, then the child's play has a mathematical focus and a comment from you about matching shapes would be appropriate and not interruptive.

After the Play: Promoting Reflection

Opportunities for children to reflect on their play are particularly important after children have encountered mathematical concepts through play. In *Early Mathematics: Promoting Good Beginnings* by NCTM and NAEYC, the authors assert, "Experiences and intuitive ideas become truly mathematical as the children reflect on them, represent them in various ways, and connect them to other ideas."

These reflections are simple to incorporate into the learning day. For example, immediately following a center choice time, children who have spent time duplicating patterns could be asked to verbally describe or to draw one of the patterns they made. If a child has just finished creating a red-blue-purple pattern of buttons, you could ask how she knew when it was time to put a red button in the pattern. Children who have spent time creating sets of nine at the math manipulatives table could be asked to describe how they made sure there were nine in each set.

Identifying Goals for Mathematics Learning

Based on guidance from NCTM, the Administration for Children and Families, and Marjorie Kostelnik and colleagues, important goals for mathematics learning in early childhood include the following:

- **Number Concepts and Operations**

  - Count with understanding and recognize "how many" in sets of objects

  - Associate quantities and the names of numbers with written numerals

  - Use a range of strategies to compare quantity in two sets of objects and describe the comparison with terms such as *more, less, greater than, fewer,* or *equal to*

  - Recognize that numbers or sets of objects can be combined or separated to make different numbers or sets through the grouping of objects

- **Patterns**

  - Sort, classify, and order objects by size, number, and other properties

  - Recognize, describe, and extend patterns such as sequences of sounds and shapes or simple numeric patterns

- **Geometry**

  - Recognize, name, build, draw, compare, and sort two- and three-dimensional shapes

  - Combine and separate shapes to make other shapes

  - Describe spatial relationships, such as *above, below, inside, outside, in front,* and *behind*

- **Measurement and Comparisons**

  - Compare and order objects using attributes of length, weight, and size, such as the terms *bigger, longer, taller,* and *heavier*

  - Use nonstandard and standard techniques and tools to measure and compare

Facilitating Mathematical Understanding through Different Types of Play

The following scenarios provide examples of how different types of play in different settings can encourage children to explore math concepts and develop skills in these areas.

In the following illustration, we see an example of guided play in which children are manipulating objects with regard to the mathematical concepts of sorting and classifying.

Guided Play for Sorting and Classifying Buttons

Mrs. Delgado calls four children over to the math table where she has placed a large set of buttons. The buttons vary in color, consisting of blue, red, and yellow. They also vary in size (small, medium, and large) and in number of holes (one, two, and three). She draws the children's attention to the buttons, saying, "Look, these buttons are in three different colors. What colors are they?" After the children reply, she asks, "How else are they different?"

Marissa says, "Some are big," and Luka adds, "These have two holes but these have three."

"And some have one hole," says Eunsook.

Mrs. Delgado gives each pair of children a box of buttons. She arranges a screen to divide the table, so each pair of children cannot see the other pair's activity. She challenges the children, saying, "Work with your partner to see if you can sort these buttons into piles. Put the ones that are alike together into piles."

Once the children have sorted most of the buttons, Mrs. Delgado says, "Okay, let's lift the screen and see what you did. You all found a way to sort the buttons. Great! First let's all look at Eunsook and Jaya's piles. Eunsook and Jaya, tell us why these buttons go together." Mrs. Delgado repeats this process for each pile. She does not point out or correct any inconsistencies, but if the children note an inconsistency, she asks them to explain their thinking to one another.

Next, she points to Marissa and Luka's side of the table. "Marissa and Luka also found a way to sort the buttons. Their way is different." She then repeats the questions she asked of the first pair, encouraging the children to listen to one another. After Marissa and Luka have explained their groupings, Mrs.

Delgado challenges the children again. "Show me a different way you could sort your buttons." If children become stuck, Mrs. Delgado might choose to model an idea by asking, "What if we put all the buttons with three holes together?" Mrs. Delgado might also provide counting practice by encouraging the children to count how many buttons are in each pile. For the third sorting, she encourages the children to sort still another way and enthusiastically tells them that she will return in a few minutes to see what they have done.

In this example, Mrs. Delgado has initiated a play activity by encouraging children to consider the multiplication possibilities that are inherent in this set of buttons. After guiding children toward playing in this way, she leaves them to pursue the button play in their own ways.

In the following scenario, we see an illustration of guided play in which children use non-standard units of measurement to determine the length of the individual cement squares that make up the patio area outside the backdoor of their classroom.

OBSERVE AND LEARN:
Guided Play for Measurement and Comparison

Miss Patel provides a few small metal buckets, each containing a large number of pennies. (You could also use other small uniform objects of sufficient weight and stability that they won't be easily scattered.) She tells the children that she is wondering how many pennies it will take to measure the length of each cement patio square. She also wonders whether the patio squares are all the same length. "Can you find out?" she asks them.

A group of children eagerly get to work measuring the cement squares. Some children work in pairs, some work independently, and some consult with peers. Miss Patel keeps an eye on the activity but does not intervene. After a few moments she tells them, "When you are finished measuring your square, tell me how long it is—how many pennies long." As children finish measuring and report to her, she gives them the option of writing the numeral in chalk next to their pennies or asking her to write it for them.

When everyone has finished, she points out either that all of the measurements are the same or that they are not the same. (The cement tiles are uniform in size, so varying measurements create an interesting question.) She asks the children, "What do you think about that?" If children note discrepancies, Miss Patel asks them how they could figure it out. If the children don't think of it themselves, she suggests recounting and/or making sure the pennies are lined up end to end. When this has finished, Miss Patel encourages those children who are interested to see how long two squares would be. She adds that during afternoon center time they will have a chance to measure the math table and other spaces in the classroom, if they would like. "And tomorrow," she adds, "we can figure out how many pennies it takes to measure the length of each one of you!"

To adapt an activity like this one for a child who has a disability that causes difficulty with motor control, the teacher could provide measuring objects that are easier to pick up, such as checkers. If sitting independently is not possible, the teacher could either provide bolsters so the child is able to participate on the ground or could provide a cardboard square the same size as a patio tile and place it on the child's wheelchair tray.

This next illustration is an example of solitary pretend free play in which a child independently includes mathematical thinking in her play.

OBSERVE AND LEARN:
Free Play Related to Number Concepts and Operations

Charlotte is playing in the sandbox, pretending to make birthday cupcakes. She has filled each cup of a large muffin pan with damp sand and has carefully tamped each down to make it solidly packed. "Cupcakes for my friends," she says to herself in a soft voice, then she counts the twelve cupcakes as she points to each one. After she has counted the cupcakes, she scoops acorns from a bucket nearby, placing one in the center of each cupcake. As she places each acorn, she repeats, "One chocolate kiss for you." Next, she breaks several twigs into small pieces. She sticks three twig pieces into each cupcake, then checks her work by counting, "One, two, three candles," for each cupcake. On the twelfth, noticing that she has placed only two candles, she exclaims, "Uh oh," and finds another small twig. She sticks it in the last cupcake, saying, "Three!"

In this episode of pretend play, Charlotte is practicing her ability to count with meaning. She is applying her counting skills within a situation that is purposeful for her and seems to be having fun as she does so. She is also demonstrating, to anyone who happens to be watching, her understanding of the principles of counting with meaning. Children can often demonstrate their understandings through their play much more accurately than they can demonstrate in other contexts. If Charlotte's teacher was watching, she has learned something important about what Charlotte knows.

Creating Play Plans to Support Mathematical Learning

Guided-Play Plan

Before the Play: Acting as Planner

Let's imagine that you have created collections of items for children to use for sorting and patterning. As a common activity in your classroom, the children know that when they have chosen or been assigned to the math-tub center, they should choose a collection and await your instructions. Children know that they can work individually, in pairs, or as a small group at this center.

Goals

The basic goals for this particular center remain the same from day to day, to provide children with continuing practice in the important fundamental math skills of sorting; classifying; and ordering objects by size, number and other properties. They also have opportunities to recognize, describe, and extend patterns such as sequences of sounds and shapes or simple numeric patterns.

Setting and Time

Let's say you have set up your daily schedule to include a forty-five-minute session during the morning for rotating centers. During this period, children engage in one of three options for fifteen minutes: math-tub center, guided small-group activity, and any other center in the classroom. After fifteen minutes, they rotate to the next option. This period provides you with some time to conduct a small-group activity and also facilitate the math-tub center. This period does not replace your free-choice center time, which is of longer duration. The math-tub center consists of ample rug space next to a low shelf, on which the tubs are stored.

Preparation and Materials

On any given day, there are ten collections in the math-tub center from which children may choose. Each collection is stored in a clear plastic tub, so children can easily identify the collection with which they want to play. Currently the collections you have available in the center are as follows:

- Pompoms in several sizes and colors
- Metal washers of various sizes
- Unifix cubes
- Small farm animals
- Small cars of various styles

- Small dinosaurs of various types
- Assorted polished stones
- Assorted beads
- 2-inch fabric swatches in various prints
- A variety of unshelled nuts*

Of course, follow your center's rules about nuts. If a child has a nut allergy, do not use.

Trays are available for children to work on if they wish. Other collections are periodically rotated in and out to keep the materials fresh and intriguing.

Provocations

Before children start their play at the math-tub center, you begin by providing them an example of a pattern. Today you use music as your medium: You tell the children to listen carefully and then play three notes on a small xylophone and repeat this pattern three times. Then you play the same three-note sequence three times again, this time saying as you strike each note, "a-b-c, a-b-c, a-b-c." "What kind of a pattern is this?" you ask the children. The children reply, "a-b-c." "That's right. Today your challenge is to create an a-b-c pattern with your collection. Make it repeat at least three times. You can work together. Come tap me on the arm when you are ready to show me." You then leave to facilitate activity at the small-group table.

During the Play: Acting as Guide

In a few moments, you return to the math-tub center to check on the children's activity. If the a-b-c pattern is new to the children, or they show that they are having difficulty, you may decide to model this pattern again, either using the musical-note pattern and saying "a-b-c, a-b-c, a-b-c," or by selecting one of the object collections not in use and using that to demonstrate.

As the children work, use a variety of questions to encourage them to examine their thinking. "What kind of pattern did you make?" "How do you know?" "If you continue your a-b-c pattern, what will come next?"

If children have made an error in their pattern, encourage them to notice and fix it. "Let's see, can you point to the first 'a'? Now show me the 'b,' then the 'c.' What's next?" Pause, using silence and attentive presence to help children notice their own errors. Encourage pairs to figure out together how to correct their pattern.

You may want to try a fill-in-the-blank strategy if children are having difficulty. For example, use the children's materials to create an a-b-c, a-b-c, a _ _ sequence, and help the children to figure out what comes next.

When children have successfully completed an example of three repetitions of an a-b-c pattern, provide suggestions for using their remaining time in the math-tub center. For example, "You made an a-b-c pattern! If you like, you can make a new a-b-c pattern or another kind of pattern. You can sort your collection into categories or count objects or play with your collection in some other way."

This example shows both an opportunity for children to practice something they can do on their own and to try something that they are unable to do without scaffolding. Scaffolding is all about providing a child the support she needs to stretch up on her tiptoes just a bit and do something she is unable to do without that "just right" support. Children can't spend all of their learning time "on their tiptoes." That would be exhausting! Children don't spend all of their learning time practicing, either. That would become boring.

One way to provide well-tuned support is to think in advance about one or two potential ways to simplify an activity once it is in progress and one or two ways to make it more challenging. In the above situation, you could challenge a child by suggesting a more difficult pattern to make, such as a-b-c-c, a-b-c-c, a-b-c-c. If a child seems to need something less challenging, you could suggest that she try a simpler pattern such as a-b, a-b, a-b, provide an a-b-c pattern for her to copy directly, or encourage her to sort the materials instead.

After the Play: Promoting Reflection

Over time, you could collect photographs of the children's patterns into a "workbook." At the top of each page, put a photograph of a pattern created by children in the math-tub center. Below that, provide spaces designated for children to draw their own patterns—or make them with stickers—of the same type as the pattern in the photograph at the top of the page. The workbook can be photocopied so each child has her own in which to practice making patterns.

Free-Play Plan

Before the Play: Acting as Planner

Let's imagine that your block center is well-equipped with a large set of classic wood unit blocks. You have learned that your block center is a ripe area for productive construction play involving mathematical concepts, and you provide daily opportunities for children to engage in free play. Today three children are in the block center. They are working together on a construction and are encountering mathematical concepts related to length, part-whole relationships, and shapes as they play.

Goals
Among the many possible explorations available in this activity are such mathematical skills as the following:

- Combining and separating shapes to make other shapes

- Comparing and ordering objects using attributes of length, weight, and size, using terms such as *bigger, longer, taller,* and *heavier*

- Recognizing, naming, building, drawing, comparing, and sorting two- and three-dimensional shapes

Setting and Time
It is now morning free-choice time, a sixty-minute daily period during which children may choose to play at any center. They are also free to move from one center to another as they choose, within your established limits on the number of children allowed in a center at one time. You have a posted limit of four children in the block center; this is based on the amount of space available in the center, as well as the number of unit blocks available. In the past, when you have allowed six children in this center, conflicts over space and materials were too frequent. Four seems to be the right limit in the block center for your class.

Preparation and Materials

Your set of unit blocks is large and basic. There are also a few architectural-detail blocks, including turrets and arched doors, but you have elected to use the available space to provide a good-sized set of the more basic unit blocks so that children can build large structures without the frustration of inadequate materials. There are not so many blocks that children do not need to share and compromise, but there are enough to avoid frequent conflicts. Your program invested resources several years ago in providing a large set of blocks for each preschool classroom. Although they are expensive, they last for generations and are an indispensable learning tool.

Provocations

The blocks themselves serve as a provocation. You have also included on the shelves in the block area a few accessories that suggest possibilities for pretend play, such as small cars and small people figures. Today, before the children began their free play period, you provided a couple of intentional visual provocations. To potentially draw children's attention to part-whole relationships, you placed a few blocks on the rug such that two 1-unit blocks are lined up atop a 2-unit block, and two 2-unit blocks are lined up atop a 4-unit block. You have also placed two triangle blocks together to form a square and two elongated triangles or "wedge" blocks together to create a rectangle.

During the Play: Acting as Guide

Observe: From where you are standing in the middle of the room, you notice that the three children are playing together in the block center, creating a wall to surround a fort. They start out with the 4-unit blocks. With these blocks, they create the bottom layer of their square enclosure wall and get halfway around with the second layer. "Here, use these next!" instructs Nick, as he picks up a couple of shorter 2-unit blocks. The children continue to add to the wall using those blocks until they run out.

Paraphrase: Casey says, "I'll get these ones," as he pulls some 1-unit blocks from the shelf. You casually paraphrase, saying "You're getting the 1-unit blocks now," as the building of the wall continues. By saying this, you are providing math vocabulary that could help the children communicate about their play, and you are drawing their attention to the "1-unit-ness" of the blocks.

Add materials: When the 1-unit blocks have run out and there is still a section of wall remaining to complete, Nick picks up two right-triangle blocks and tries to set them together on the wall to substitute for a 1-unit block, but they slide apart. You offer Nick some masking tape to stick the two triangle blocks together: "Will this help?" This serves to consolidate his understanding that two right-triangle blocks can be put together to make a square.

To offer a lower and less direct level of assistance, before providing any tape you might say, "I wonder how you could get those two triangles to stay together—any ideas?" On the other hand, a higher and more direct level of assistance would be offered if you said, "Here is some tape. You can use it to stick the two triangles together to make a square."

After the Play: Promoting Reflection

Of course, it is not necessary to follow up on every play episode with documentation and reflection. Occasional reflection and representation, however, help children to think about their play and help you to think about how to support their play. Here are some potential follow-ups for this one.

Documentation

Make brief notes about what knowledge each child displayed regarding length, parts and whole, and combining shapes. Was there anything that seemed to confuse them? What play provocations might you provide in the next few days to help them move forward with their understanding?

Reflection and Representation

You could encourage these children to create a resource book about unit blocks. If they seem interested, you might suggest that they draw pictures or take photographs to illustrate the following concepts:

- One small rectangle is equal to two square blocks; in other words, one 2-unit block equals two 1-unit blocks.

- Two right-triangle blocks are equal to one square 1-unit block.

  The resource book can be kept on the shelf in the block center.

As you reflect on the activity, think about the following questions:

- How did the children respond to the provocations I provided? What did they do and/or say?

- What support strategies did I use? How did the children respond to my support strategies? What did they do and/or say?

- What evidence did I see or hear that children were moving in the direction of my identified goal?

- What might I do differently, if I were to implement this or a similar plan again?

- What will my next step be, with regard to helping the children move toward this goal?

Create Your Own Play Plan

Use the template provided below. Start with one or two mathematical learning goals, which you can identify from the list provided in this chapter, from your state's early learning standards, or from the curriculum you use. Then, based on your knowledge of the children you teach—including their interests, their abilities, and the kinds of things they like to play—think about how to create a play plan that helps children move toward each goal. Refer to chapter 1 to remind yourself of the many different types of play that you may provide for and encourage. Refer to chapter 3 to remind yourself about possible support roles and strategies you may use to support children's play with regard to the goals you identified.

Before the Play

Goals

_____

_____

Setting and Time

_____

_____

Preparation and Materials

_____

_____

Provocations

_____

_____

During the Play

Possible Support Strategies

_____

_____

After the Play

Documentation

_____

_____

Reflection and Representation

_____

_____

seven [7]

Fostering Language Learning and Literacy

During the preschool years, children's language development grows by leaps and bounds. Also during these years, children's understanding of basic concepts related to emergent literacy has great potential to flourish. Neither language nor emergent literacy grows in a vacuum, however. Both are closely linked to the kinds of experiences children have and the environment by which they are surrounded. In fact, oral language development and emergent literacy are very closely linked, and that is why they are presented together in this chapter. Just as language develops through interactions in a conversation-rich social environment, literacy emerges through social interactions in an environment rich with print, people making meaning from print, and people using print to communicate words and ideas.

The growth of emergent literacy in the early years rests on the foundation provided by oral language development. Learning to understand and communicate through oral language is a critical step toward eventually learning to read and write. This makes perfectly good sense—because literacy is the ability to communicate and draw meaning from marks on a page that represent spoken language, then of course language is an indispensable basic ingredient.

The pace of typical language development during the preschool years is astonishing. Did you know that between the ages of two and six years, children in general learn about ten thousand words? On average, preschoolers' vocabulary grows at the rate of five words per day. In addition to vocabulary, preschoolers learn a great deal about the rules of language. They learn the rules of *syntax*, which refers to how words are put together into a sentence to convey meaning. They learn the rules of *morphology*, which refers to how words are altered to show singular and plural, past and present tense, and so on. They also learn the rules of conversation, such as when and how to listen, how to take turns in conversation, how to combine words with body language and tone of voice to enhance meaning, and how to use questions for different conversational purposes. Although these things are not simply directly taught to preschoolers through planned instruction, none of it happens by magic either. The ease with which children learn language is dependent on their social and linguistic environment and experiences. Adults who use rich language with children and hold conversations with them about things that hold meaning and interest for them have a strong influence on the progression of young children's language development.

As human beings, we communicate a great deal through the spoken word. The attainment of literacy tremendously expands our possibilities for communication, both expressive and receptive. Children can learn many fundamental literacy-related concepts and skills during the preschool years. These include the understanding that print conveys meaning, letters correspond to sounds, and in English we read from left to right. These also include the ability to name letters and to develop awareness of such story elements as character, setting, and sequence. A variety of language and literacy goals for the early childhood years are presented on pages 98–100.

The early childhood years comprise a critical period for the development of language. They are also highly sensitive years for the development of other emerging skills that build toward the ability to read and write. As the International Reading Association

(IRA) and NAEYC assert in their 1998 joint position statement, "Although reading and writing abilities continue to develop throughout the life span, the early childhood years—from birth through age 8—are the most important period for literacy development."

The importance of early childhood for growth in language and other abilities underlying literacy does not, however, imply that we should push preschoolers to read and write. It does not mean that teaching practices common in the early years of elementary school should be pulled down into preschool classrooms. Just as with mathematical learning, there are basic understandings and abilities that must come first before children can read in the traditional sense of decoding print. According to the IRA and NAEYC joint position statement, if children are exposed to appropriate literacy experiences and teaching practices during early childhood, then "most children learn to read and write at age six or seven, a few learn at four, some learn at five, and others need intensive individualized support to learn to read at eight or nine."

In the preschool years, children are generally considered to be in Phase 1, or the Awareness and Exploration phase on the continuum of children's development in early reading and writing, according to IRA and NAEYC. This is the stage at which children engage in exploration of their environment. This is the stage at which they build the foundations of learning to read and write. Some examples of what children can generally be expected to do in this phase are listed below.

Children can:

- Enjoy listening to and discussing story books.

- Understand that print carries a message.

- Engage in reading and writing attempts.

- Identify labels and sounds in their environment.

- Participate in rhyming games.

- Identify some letters and make some letter-sound matches.

- Use letters or approximations of letters to represent written language—especially meaningful words such as their names and phrases such as "I love you."

Some preschool children may not be ready to do everything listed here, due to developmental variation, disability, or lack of experience. Some preschool children show characteristics at the next phase, which is experimental reading and writing, or beyond.

Play Is Crucial in Developing Both Language and Literacy

The most important way to support preschoolers' language development is by talking with them. Not simply talking to them, but talking with them. In other words, conversations between adults and children and between children are a wonderful way to support language growth. Conversations about activities that interest children or in which they are currently engaged often work best.

The most important way to support preschool children's literacy development is through reading books that interest them. Sometimes this means reading to them. Sometimes this means reading with them, as the adult points things out in the illustrations, responds to children's comments, and asks or answers questions. Sometimes this means listening as a child pages through a book, points to pictures, and "reads" what he recalls of the text to you. Sometimes all three of these reading processes occur within the sharing of a single book.

Conversations and shared reading are both excellent strategies for supporting children's language development and literacy learning. There are many other effective strategies with which to accompany these, such as the following:

- Talk about letters by name and sounds.

- Establish a literacy-rich environment, stocked with lots of books, environmental print, and literacy tools such as paper and markers.

- Include many books with predictable text, including repetition and rhyme.

- Reread books that children enjoy.

- Encourage children to draw, print, and write.

- Engage children in language games, such as games that play with sounds.

- Promote literacy-related play activities.

- Encourage children to talk about ideas and events that are important to them.

Several of the strategies listed are play or activities that can be readily embedded in play. While play alone is not recommended as the only way to develop preschoolers' emergent literacy, a very large body of research supports that children's play contributes in many ways to the development of language and literacy. Play promotes oral language development; the development of phonological awareness, which is the conscious awareness of the sounds of language; print awareness; and general knowledge. Research has shown that all of these abilities are predictive of children's literacy development. Blended approaches that combine play with more structured approaches are recommended. Play alone is not enough, but play and playful activities are indispensable ingredients for promoting preschoolers' language and literacy development.

Strategies for Supporting Language and Literacy Development

Provide and show children how to use puzzles, games, and other materials that let them practice recognizing and naming letters, matching letters with sounds, and matching words with the letters that represent their beginning sounds. Possibilities include the following:

- Alphabet puzzles

- Large magnetic or foam letters

- Alphabet matching games

- Beginning-sounds puzzles

- Letter-sorting boxes

Remember to demonstrate to children how to use all of these. They may decide to use the materials for other playful and productive purposes, which is fine in the context of play. But don't assume that children will figure out on their own how to use these for the manufacturers' intended purposes.

While children play with the materials described above, look for opportunities to support and challenge their thinking. For example, "Yes, *ball* starts with the letter *B*. What sound does the letter *B* make?" and "What else starts with the *B* sound?"

Preschool children are often fascinated by their own printed names and are interested in how their names look in comparison to other names. With this in mind, you could create a name-recognition matching game. Make one set of cards with a photo of a classmate on each, and another set of cards with a child's name clearly printed on each. Encourage children to work together to figure out which printed name goes with which photo. If children have difficulty recognizing a name, draw their attention to the beginning letter. Ask them what sound that letter makes. If needed, demonstrate making the sound, and challenge the children to figure out whose name begins with that sound.

Provide literacy materials in a variety of classroom centers where play occurs. These materials can include alphabet cookie cutters with the clay or playdough; letter stamps of various types in the art center; and paper, books, newspapers, magazines, and writing utensils in the dramatic play and blocks centers. Demonstrate possibilities for using these materials. A child can use letter stamps to put his name on an art creation; markers and paper can be used to make a grocery list. Provide newspapers and magazines that the children can "read" in a home-themed or airplane-themed dramatic play episode.

Occasionally provide dramatic play opportunities with literacy-related themes. Possibilities include library, post office, classroom, and bookstore. Provide background experiences (possibly through field trips), information about roles and possible activities, and props to support children's literacy-themed play. Keep in mind that dramatic play can occur in many places outside of the designated dramatic play center—in the block center, on the playground, at the dollhouse, in a puppet center, or at a table with small blocks and people figures.

Engage children in rhyming games, such as inserting a rhyming word in place of a word in a familiar song or nursery rhyme. For example, after children become familiar with "Twinkle, Twinkle, Little Star," help them identify a word that rhymes with star and a word that rhymes with sky. Then insert these into the song. As a playful and often funny game, some silliness is okay. The name game is a similar possibility. In the name game, a child's name is altered by inserting her name (minus the beginning sound) into the chant. For example, using my name the chant would be:

> Kristen, Kristen, bo bisten.
>
> Bo nana fana, fo fisten.
>
> My name is Kristen.
>
> Kristen.

Using Conversation to Expand Vocabulary and Grammatical Understanding

During all kinds of play, and in a variety of play situations, be on the lookout for opportunities to expand children's vocabulary, especially vocabulary related to aspects of the play that are important to them. When opportunities arise, children are often very open and motivated to learn new words. For example, when a child refers to a block in his structure as the "door block," you could say, "Good idea to use that arch-shaped block for a door." Notice that this mini-lesson is done within the flow of the child's play, without distracting him from his own purposes and in a way that honors the importance of the child's play.

Describing and paraphrasing are two language-support strategies that can fit naturally into play. With the first, you can simply describe what you see in the children's play activity while inserting the new vocabulary word, as in, "Jason is *jiggling* the keys," or "You made a *coil* with clay." When paraphrasing, you repeat some of what a child has just said, inserting a new word or phrase. For example, when a child says, "I'm cooking eggs in this pot," you could comment, "I see! You are cooking eggs in a *skillet*. They look delicious."

Paraphrasing is also an excellent strategy to use during play to enhance children's grammatical learning. Consider Leila, who is playing at the dollhouse, creating a scenario in which the children are playing outside and climbing trees. "Oh, no," Leila exclaims, "he falled out of the tree!" This is a perfect opportunity to support Leila's grammatical learning within a fun play activity and without detracting from the play. How might you use paraphrase reflection here? One good possibility is: "Oh! He fell out of the tree! Do you need an ambulance?" With these words, you have provided the correct form and still kept the focus on the child's play activity. You have even suggested a pretend possibility for Leila to consider: Call an ambulance!

When children are engaged in various kinds of play, there are many opportunities to encourage conversation by asking them to describe what they are doing. This can be done with a simple descriptive comment, such as, "You've got all the trucks lined up." This shows your interest and attention without demanding a response from the child. The child can engage with you if he chooses. A more direct way of inviting conversation would be, for example, "I see pink and blue in your painting. Would you like to tell me about it?" or simply, "I would love to hear about your painting." You can use your judgment in deciding when to use such strategies. Too many of such invitations during play can feel to the child like an intrusion.

Identifying Goals for Language and Literacy Development

Marjorie Kostelnik et al., the IRA and NAEYC, and the Administration for Children and Families offer lists of recommended goals for young children as they develop language and emergent literacy skills. Those goals include the following:

■ **Listening**

  ▪ Demonstrating courteous listening behaviors

  ▪ Identifying sounds in their environment

- Increasing their receptive vocabulary

- Demonstrating the awareness that spoken language is composed of smaller segments of sound

■ **Speaking**

- Articulating their ideas, intents, emotions, and desires

- Asking and answering questions

- Creating and describing imaginative situations

- Increasing their expressive vocabulary

- Using increasingly complex sentence structure

- Understanding, following, and using appropriate social and conversational rules

- Understanding and using a wide variety of words for a variety of purposes

■ **Writing**

- Recognizing that they can convey messages to others through written symbols (drawing and writing)

- Understanding that speech can be preserved through writing

- Observing and imitating writing

- Connecting letter sounds to graphemes (the letters of the alphabet)

- Generating graphemes

- Putting their thoughts on paper, first through simple pictures and then incorporating print into their drawings

- Using their own temporary versions of writing, working gradually toward conventional spelling, punctuation, and format (left to right, top to bottom, spacing)

- Demonstrating an understanding of how print is used (functions of print)

- Demonstrating an understanding of the rules that govern how print works (conventions of print)

- Writing for a variety of purposes using increasingly sophisticated marks

■ **Reading**

- Recognizing graphemes

- Recognizing that they can get meaning from print

- Practicing reading-like behavior, moving from pretend reading to attempting to match the flow of their language with book illustrations and with print

- Responding to written symbols in the environment, such as their names and others' names, signs, advertisements, and labels

- Predicting, on the basis of information in the text and their personal life experiences, what will come next in stories that are being read

- Developing an understanding of story elements and structure, such as story sequence, main ideas, characters, setting, and plot development

- Creating new endings for stories, drawing on logical elements of the original stories

- Developing a sight vocabulary

- Identifying letters of the alphabet

- Producing correct sounds associated with letters

- Demonstrating an understanding of narrative structure through storytelling and retelling

Facilitating Language and Literacy Development through Different Types of Play

In the following illustration, we see an example of guided play in which children are taught to play a game that consists of matching letter and picture cards.

OBSERVE AND LEARN:
Identifying Letters and Letter Sounds

Ms. Caitlin sees that Marta and Delaney are finishing up a table game, and she decides this is a good time to introduce the new matching game that she has brought in. The game consists of a set of cards with pictures of familiar objects to be matched with a set that has a letter of the alphabet on each card.

"Look what I've got, girls. It's a matching game with letters and pictures. Make two piles: one with all of the letters, and one with all of the pictures. After you do that, I'll come back and show you how to play."

Once she sees that the cards are sorted, Ms. Caitlin returns and helps the children lay the cards out so that the letter cards are turned face-down. "I'll pick a card first," says Ms. Caitlin, as she draws a letter card and turns it over. "Do you know the name of this letter?" If the girls have difficulty naming it, she gives a few hints such as, "Take a look at the alphabet chart on the wall to see if you can figure it out," "It's the second letter in the alphabet," or "It's the first letter in Beth's name," or simply, "This is the letter B." She asks the girls what sound the letter B makes and helps them figure it out or directly demonstrates for them as needed.

To avoid helping too much, and to keep the game at a comfortable but motivating level of challenge, Ms. Caitlin tries to give the least direct support possible at first. She then increases her support if the girls cannot do it on their own. Once the girls have named the letter and identified its sound, Ms. Caitlin makes the /b/ sound several times for the girls. She encourages them to make the /b/ sound themselves, then says, "Now see if you can find the matching picture—the one that starts with the sound /b/. I'll come back in a little while and see if you found it!" When she returns, she instructs the girls to take turns at flipping over a letter card and to work together to identify the letter and its sound and find the matching picture.

This type of game is a good way for a teacher to begin to see which children can name which letters, how well they can associate letters with sounds, and whether they can identify beginning sounds in words. By making notes, the teacher can see which children need additional support in this area.

Simple games and activities can offer children fun opportunities to practice their developing language and literacy skills. In the following example, we see a whole group of children, under the guidance of their teacher, engage in a popular singing game designed to enhance their awareness that words are composed of units of sound.

Every Monday morning, Mr. Ramsey leads the children in singing "Willoughby Wallaby." This is a good greeting song because it is a way to say everyone's name and give group attention to each individual child, plus it starts the morning on a happy note.

Mr. Ramsey begins singing as the children are settling into their places. "Willoughby Wallaby wee. . . ," he sings, and the children quickly respond with "an elephant sat on me." "Willoughby Wallaby woo . . ." "An elephant sat on you." The song continues in turn-taking fashion as Mr. Ramsey includes a rhyme for each child's name:

> MR. R: Willoughby Wallaby Wicardo, an elephant sat on . . .
> CHILDREN: Ricardo!
> MR. R: Willoughby Wallaby Wegan, an elephant sat on . . .
> CHILDREN: Megan!

In addition to providing children with practice in listening to language sounds and rhyme and practice in segmenting out the first sound from the rest of the name, this song allows Mr. Ramsey an opportunity to see which children seem to struggle with these skills and which are beginning to master them.

Phonological awareness underlies children's ability to learn the relationship between letters and sounds. Research has shown that it is one of the strongest predictors of later reading success.

After-Play Reflection Time

In previous chapters, we have looked at examples of teachers encouraging children to reflect upon their play and to represent their play through pictures and writing. This process can enhance many kinds of play and provide children language- and literacy-rich opportunities to think, talk, draw, and write about something that is highly meaningful and relevant to them.

In this example, Mrs. Murphree has encouraged children to exercise their representational abilities with regard to a meaningful subject: their own play. She has gained a window to individual children's feelings and thoughts about their play. This experience enables Mrs. Murphree's planning for future play, and reflecting on their own play can spark children's ideas for future play.

Creating Play Plans to Support Language and Literacy Development

Guided-Play Plan

Before the Play: Acting as Planner

Let's imagine that Theo is in the process of being assessed for ASD. As is typically the case for children on the autism spectrum, Theo has difficulty with social relationships, play, and communication. Often when he ventures into the dramatic play center, misunderstandings erupt into conflicts. You want to create a social-play experience that can help Theo engage with other children in this center. You have heard about using guided dramatic-play experiences based on simple familiar stories, and you decide to implement a version of this. You recognize that other children can gain from this experience as well, though the goals for them may be different from the goals you have for Theo.

Goals

For Theo, your immediate objective is to provide him the experience of successfully and enjoyably playing with other children and to promote his acceptance by the other children.

For all of the children, you want them to develop an understanding of story elements and structure: story sequence, main ideas, characters, setting, and plot development. You also want them to demonstrate an understanding of narrative structure through storytelling and retelling.

Setting and Time

You decide to implement these play sessions in the dramatic play center during your center rotation time. For several days, the dramatic play center will be used only for this purpose.

Preparation and Materials

You will be devoting much of your attention to this activity during center rotation for these several days, so you have provided activities at the other centers that children will be able to engage in with minimum help from you.

You select a book that will be the basis for the guided dramatic play. The book needs to be a very simple one with several characters and a repetitive structure. You consider several: *Three Billy Goats Gruff, The Three Little Pigs, Goldilocks and the Three Bears,* and *The Little Red Hen*. You decide on *The Little Red Hen* because it involves bread, one of Theo's favorite things to eat.

You gather simple props to support this play: a kerchief for the little red hen, dog ears for the dog, cat ears for the cat, a duck-bill hat for the duck, seeds, something to cut the wheat, a bundle of tall grasses to represent wheat, a basket, real or pretend bread, and an oven, which could be a box or the oven from the dramatic play center.

Provocations

You read the story of *The Little Red Hen* to the children several times over the course of a week, gradually encouraging them to chime in and say the lines with you:

HEN: "Who will help me plant these seeds?"

"Not I," said the cat.

"Not I," said the dog.

"Not I," said the duck.

HEN: "Then I will do it by myself."

As the children become good at reciting all of the lines, tell them that next week you will help them create a play about the Little Red Hen with props and costumes.

During the Play: Acting as Guide

Consider the following possible support strategies. Create groups of four children, and ask one to be the narrator and the others to be three of the characters. Or, you may serve as the narrator. You might initially assign children to characters according to their capabilities and then switch roles as the whole group gains competence.

For the group including Theo, you carefully select peers who are cooperative and helpful and have good play skills.

As you talk about the drama, use vocabulary words such as *character, setting,* and *story sequence.*

Provide a flannel board, felt characters and props, and *The Little Red Hen* book so that children have the option to practice the story on their own or in pairs during free-choice time.

Help children remember when to use their props, as needed. You can also encourage the more competent children to remind their peers who need reminding. Keep in mind that scaffolding is not only provided by adults. More competent peers can often provide effective support to their peers who may need it. Children may be able to come up with helpful support on their own, or you may need to suggest it directly with words like these: "Sherry, sometimes Theo forgets that he is the dog. You can remind him by gently tapping him on the arm and whispering, 'You are the dog, Theo. It's your turn.'"

After the Play: Promoting Reflection

Documentation
After children have gained confidence and can enact the story well, you could videotape several of them and show the recordings to the class. These could also be posted online for family members to view, or you may even show them at a family spaghetti-dinner night at the school. Children can create tickets, signs, and even programs showing the cast of characters.

Reflection and Representation
Individual children can be encouraged to draw, write, and/or dictate about each step in the story sequence. Laminate the children's individual drawings, and offer them as a sequencing activity. Children can take turns or work together to arrange the class-created pages into the narrative sequence of the story.

Free-Play Plan

Before the Play: Acting as Planner

Let's imagine that your local library holds a monthly preschool story time. Your preschool class enjoys this excursion. They have been excited about the lively storytelling, book reading, and puppet shows they have seen and participated in at the library. Recently, you have noticed a few of the children pretending to check out books in the reading center of your classroom. You decide to support and build upon this interest by creating a library-themed dramatic play center.

Goals
Through play with books and library-themed props, the children will create and describe imaginative situations. As they look at and talk about books, they will have opportunities to demonstrate an understanding of how print is used and the rules that govern how print works, as well as practice reading-like behavior. Through signs, check-out cards, and other materials, they will be able to respond to written symbols in the environment.

Setting and Time
This center will be available to children during their two forty-five–minute free-choice periods. You decide to reorganize a bit in your classroom to accommodate this by placing the book center next to the dramatic play center so that both can be used in the play. The dramatic play center is next to the gathering place on the rug, so that area could also be used by the children as a place for conducting their own story time, similar to the story times at the local library.

Preparation and Materials
After removing some materials from the dramatic play center, such as kitchen items and dress-up clothes, you add library-related props such as in the list that follows. You decide to add only a few basics to begin with. You can add more over a week or so, as children's play develops.

- Date stamper

- Large sticky notes, to put inside books for stamping dates

- Old credit cards or gift cards to use as library cards

- Additional books

- Books in Mandarin, borrowed from Liang's family

- Old computer keyboard and perhaps a screen

- Pens and pads of paper

- Desk to check out books

- Bags in which to put books

- Box for book returns

- Empty CD and DVD cases

- Puppets in rug-story area

- Signs such as Check Out, Book Return, Big Books, Small Books, CDs, DVDs, Quiet Please, and so on

Provocations
Prior to setting up the library dramatic play center, you could make arrangements for a brief small-group, behind-the-scenes tour of the library on your next trip to

story time. Suggest to the person conducting the tour that he (or you) point out the roles that people play in a library, some common things that people say, and common actions and interactions that happen in the library. Take some photos while you are there, which can be placed in the dramatic play center to remind children of the possibilities.

You can read a book about libraries, such as *The Library* by Sarah Stewart, which describes how the character Elizabeth creates her own library to accommodate her many books. Show children the photos you took on your visit to the library, and ask them to recall what they saw and heard on their tour.

During the Play: Acting as Guide

Consider the following possible support strategies: Point out the Mandarin books you have included. Better yet, encourage Liang, a dual language learner whose home language is Mandarin, to point out the books. Help children to see how the print is different from the print in English books, the words sound different, and the print is organized differently on the page.

Add materials. Maybe the signs could be introduced several days into the play. Start with just a few signs. Encourage the children to try to figure out what each sign says. You can direct their attention to the first letter. They can also decide where to put each sign. Children can suggest what additional signs might be needed, and you can help them to create these.

Ask the children whether they know what the markings made by the date stamps mean and the purpose in stamping a date in the book. If they do not know, provide them with that information. You could then provide a new pretend possibility: What will happen if someone returns his book two days late?

Prompt the children to consider rules for their library, such as the number of books that a person can check out at one time. Guide them to consider that they might need a sign to remind everyone about that rule.

Keep in mind the potential goals you thought of initially. If, after several days, children get stuck in only going through the basic motions of library activity, you can guide them toward incorporating some imaginative situations into their play. Model a new role, or introduce a fun book about the library. One option, *Arthur Locked in the Library!* by Marc Brown, is a chapter book in which Arthur and Francine get locked in (you guessed it!) the library after hours and must find a way out.

After the Play: Promoting Reflection

Documentation
This play option may remain interesting and valuable over several weeks. During that time, you could make notes of things children do or say that are evidence that they are progressing toward the goals you set for this activity. Display your notes for par-

ents and others to see, so they can appreciate the importance of this play activity. Notes could be displayed on a bulletin board, in a newsletter, or on a webpage.

Reflection and Representation
At the end of the first week, ask the children to think and talk about what they like best about playing in the library. Prompt them to consider some different things they could play within the library theme next week. This brief conversation might bring to mind some additional props or other supports you could add.

Reflect on the children's play as you ask yourself the following questions:

- How did the children respond to the provocations I provided? What did they do or say?

- What support strategies did I use? How did the children respond to my support strategies? What did they do or say?

- What evidence did I see or hear that children were moving in the direction of my identified goals?

- What might I do differently, if I were to implement this or a similar plan again?

- What will my next step be with regard to helping the children move toward this goal?

Create Your Own Play Plan

Before the Play

Goals

_____

_____

Setting and Time

_____

_____

Preparation and Materials

_____

_____

Provocations

_____

_____

During the Play

Possible Support Strategies

_____

_____

After the Play

Documentation

_____

_____

_____

Reflection and Representation

_____

_____

_____

eight [8]

Supporting Play and So Much More

So far, we have looked at how play supports development and learning in the areas of literacy, language, social competence, self-regulation, emotional development, and mathematical learning. The contribution of play to these important dimensions is considerable, and yet there is so much more! Next, let's briefly examine a few other aspects of preschoolers' learning and growth that thrive through the process of play: creativity, physical knowledge, musical learning, and motor development.

Creativity

Like play, creativity is one of those concepts that has been defined in many ways. It can be described as a flexible and fluent production of ideas that are unique, complex, or elaborate; the ability to think in unique ways, produce unusual ideas, or combine things in different ways; and the production of something original and meaningful.

E.P. Torrance, an educational psychologist who is often considered the father of creativity research, describes the creative process as consisting of several elements: fluency, flexibility, originality, and elaboration.

- ■ **Fluency:** The process of generating many different ideas. For example, name all of the spherical things you can think of in one minute. The more you name, the more fluent your thinking.

- ■ **Flexibility:** The process of generating many different ideas, with the emphasis on different. Flexibility involves the ability to change direction or think in another way. For example, in one minute name as many uses of a brick as you can think of that are very different from one another. The more different uses you come up with, the more flexible your thinking

- **Originality:** Creative thinking is characterized by originality, the process of generating ideas that are unique or unusual. For example, if asked to name unusual ways to use transparent tape, the response "to wrap a present" is not highly original. "To make windows for a dollhouse" is more original.

- **Elaboration:** Creative thinking is characterized by elaboration, the process of enhancing an idea by adding more detail. For example, the idea of using transparent tape to make a dollhouse window might be elaborated on by thinking of sticking two pieces of tape face to face so that the interior of the window will not be sticky.

OBSERVE AND LEARN:
Creative Play with Open-Ended Materials

Ms. Sara and Mr. Ray are coteachers who enjoy scavenging. They frequently browse in thrift shops, craft stores, the local repurposing center, and other sources in search of inexpensive open-ended "junk" they can use with the children as materials for creative play. The materials sets they have put together include:

- Sturdy cardboard tubes and boxes, large cardboard corner pieces used for packaging, and empty plastic coffee cans to add to the unit blocks in the block center

- Plastic rings from used tape dispensers, plastic disks and cylinders of unknown origin, bottle caps and lids, unwanted playing cards, and paint-chip samples

- Wooden craft sticks of various sizes, flat wooden shapes, and buttons

- Seashells, pinecones, acorns, small pieces of polished driftwood, and discontinued small carpet samples from a flooring store

- Stray game pieces or incomplete sets: checkers, dominos, chess pieces, dice, and so on

- Glass pebbles and smooth mosaic pieces of various colors, shapes, and sizes

- Empty thread spools, film reels, clothespins, ribbon lengths, and discarded building toy sticks

Ms. Sara and Mr. Ray occasionally provide these and similar sets of materials at the manipulatives table, in the block corner, in the dramatic play area, and at the doll house. The children exercise their fluency, flexibility, and originality by imagining and enacting various ways of using the materials in their play. The teachers support this creative behavior by showing their interest and prompting new possibilities through occasional thoughtful comments and questions: "That's a new way to use a craft stick," "I wonder what this could be," "You found a way to use the clothespins and film reels together," "How did you do that?" "Tell me about your idea," and "This looks kind of like a tiny table to me."

Why Creativity?

Creativity is important. A recent IBM poll of 1,500 CEOs identified creativity as the number one leadership competency of the future (IBM Institute for Business Value, 2016). As the global economy is shifting toward an economy that values innovation, the ability to engage in creative idea–generation and problem solving is becoming a necessary skill in both education and work.

Creativity is something that young children seem to be especially good at, and one of the best ways to nurture children's creativity is to support and protect what they already have. Play provides many opportunities for young children to flex their creative muscles. A few goals for children's creative development, which can be supported through play, are listed below. As you read, exercise your own creativity. What are some ways that play can support children's movement toward these important goals?

- Demonstrates flexibility, imagination, and inventiveness in approaching tasks and activities

- Uses creativity and imagination to manipulate materials and assume roles in dramatic play situations

- Uses a variety of materials, tools, techniques, and processes in the arts—visual art, music, dance, and drama

- Seeks multiple solutions to a question, task, or problem

Ideas for Supporting Creativity through Play

Provide many opportunities for creative art experiences in which children can use art materials in their own ways. Creative art and cookie-cutter crafts are not the same. Allow children to exercise their fluency, flexibility, originality, and elaboration in art experiences that are truly their own. For these experiences, encourage a focus on the process rather than the end product. Creative art involves exploration, experimentation, and play.

Storytelling can be a kind of play. Using a story with which children are familiar, encourage them to think of different endings for the story. Imagination questions are fun, and entice children to mentally play with ideas and possibilities: "Would it be more exciting if it went backward?" "What would happen if our pet gerbil had to wear shoes?" "What would happen if everyone looked exactly alike?" "What if our classroom were turned upside down?"

Provide loose parts. As Lisa Daly and Miriam Beloglovsky define the term in their book *Loose Parts*, these items are "alluring, beautiful found objects and materials that children can move, manipulate, control, and change while they play." Children can incorporate loose parts in their play in virtually endless ways. They can sort, create patterns and designs, build, and make pictures. They can use them for investigation and experimentation. They can elaborate on block buildings with them. They can use them as props for dramatic play. The following is a list of possible loose parts:

- Small, smooth stones
- Acorns
- Beads
- Tree cookies
- Glass pebbles
- Empty cans (cover sharp edges with duct tape)
- Bottle caps
- Leaves

- Ribbons
- Paper clips
- Cardboard
- Small tiles
- Empty thread spools
- Velcro hair rollers
- Paint-sample chips
- Discarded game pieces
- Packing material

Physical Knowledge

Physical knowledge is an aspect of cognitive development that intersects with the science of physics, mechanics, and objects in the natural world. Preschoolers really are scientists and engineers by nature! Simply put, physical knowledge is knowledge about physical phenomena. It is knowledge about the properties of objects and the laws of nature. Physical knowledge includes knowledge of such properties of objects as shape, size, color, and flexibility. It includes knowledge of how objects function: Some objects roll downhill; some objects slide downhill. It includes knowledge of how objects function under different conditions: Water takes the shape of the container in which it is placed; so does playdough, if you press it in. Physical-knowledge activities are those in which children intentionally act on objects physically and mentally to produce an effect.

For preschoolers, physical knowledge activities involve opportunities for the child to directly act upon objects and substances and to control and vary their actions. In other words, physical knowledge activities are not demonstrations conducted by a teacher. Instead, they are real, hands-on opportunities for children to learn through play about objects and their properties and about the laws of nature. Physical-knowledge activities may occur during free play, or they may be play opportunities that are initially guided by an adult. Some goals toward physical-knowledge development are as follows:

- Observes, describes, and discusses properties of materials and transformation of substances
- Explores firsthand a variety of cause-and-effect relationships

- Examines the observable properties of manufactured and natural objects using multisensory abilities

- Acquires knowledge related to the physical sciences, such as changes in matter; forces affecting motion, direction, and speed; and physical properties and characteristics of phenomena

Ideas for Supporting Physical Knowledge through Play

The sandbox, mud kitchen, and water table are places where children often engage in explorations of physical phenomena. In addition to posing questions or challenges, you can enhance the possibilities for children's physical-knowledge development in these areas by your deliberate choices and provision of materials. For example, dry sand and wet sand behave differently. Sometimes allow children to control the addition of water to the sandbox. Funnels, a turkey baster, and clear plastic tubing added to the water table can lead to discoveries about flow, pressure, and how a siphon works.

Provide ice for children to play with on a concrete sidewalk. Encourage them to see whether the ice behaves differently in the sun and in the shade. Fill empty house-paint cans with water, and allow children to use large brushes to "paint" the sidewalk or sides of the building. Ask, "What will happen if you paint three coats of water? Will it be different from one coat?"

Provide planks in the block area, and encourage children to create ramps with varying inclines. What happens when a tennis ball is placed at the top of the ramp? What happens when a marble is placed there? Is speed of the object related to its size? Is the speed related to its weight? Is speed related to the steepness of the incline? Remember, this is a play activity. Provide encouragement, ask questions to help children think, but avoid directing them.

Games such as Don't Spill the Beans can help children develop physical knowledge. In the commercial game, children take turns placing a single bean at a time on the balancing bean jar, which tips easily. The idea is to place all of your beans without tipping the jar. This activity encourages children to think about how balance works and how to create balance.

As you plan play activities for the development of physical knowledge, keep in mind the multiple senses children can use to move toward physical-knowledge goals. For example, while typical children gain a great deal of physical knowledge through sight, a child who is blind can feel and hear the way objects respond to her actions. Children can discover through touch, hearing, and even smell.

Musical Learning

Musical learning is important for every child, not just for those with special talents who may grow up to be highly skilled musicians. Music is an integral part of the pleasure of life. It is also connected to other areas of learning, including math, science, and language. There are many ways for preschool children to learn about music at school, and one very important way is through play. For those teachers who do not think of themselves as musicians, the idea of supporting children's musical learning might feel intimidating. However, when we realize that preschoolers approach musical activity as play, supporting their musical learning is something that any teacher can do! Some goals for musical learning are as follows:

- Recognizes and responds to basic elements of music, such as beat, pitch, melody, rhythm, dynamics, tempo, and mood

- Participates in musical activities such as listening, singing, performing, and creating

- Expresses what is felt and heard in various musical tempos and styles

- Experiments with musical instruments

Musical Terms

- **Beat:** The recurring rhythmic pulse underlying music; beat is a part of rhythm

- **Pitch:** Highness or lowness of a musical sound

- **Melody:** The sequence of single tones in a musical composition

- **Rhythm:** The time-based components of music; longer and shorter sounds and silences are grouped together in various ways

- **Dynamics:** The loudness and softness of musical sounds

- **Tempo:** The speed at which music is performed

- **Mood:** Combination of musical elements that evoke an emotional response

- **Timbre:** The unique qualities of sound made by a voice or instrument, enabling the listener to identify the source

Ideas for Supporting Musical Learning through Play

Provide a collection of percussion instruments with which children can play, such as a hand drum, box drum, bongo drum, doumbek, djembe, tambourine, and possibly even a variety of homemade drums. Designate an area for drum exploration. You might prefer to do this activity outdoors at a designated table or on a blanket. Encourage children to explore the different sounds the instruments can make. Which makes a louder sound? Which makes a softer sound? Which sounds do the children like, and why? Encourage the children to mimic very simple rhythm patterns. Drums, as well as other instruments with strong vibration, can also be fun for children with hearing impairments. Even children who are deaf can feel differences in vibration and rhythm.

Provide two sets of hand bells, and encourage children to match up the pairs that sound alike—bells that have the same pitch. Typically, hand bells are color-coded for pitch. To make this more challenging, you can paint all of the bells the same color, so children will only be able to rely on pitch comparison.

Provide opportunities for children to play freely at dancing and moving with music. Use different types of music—a waltz, only drums, fast music, slow music, music with different moods, and so on. A few simple props, such as silky scarfs or streamers, are often encouraging to children, as are attentive comments such as, "You're moving very smoothly!" or "Does this music make you want to jump?" Join in yourself if you feel like it!

This listening-and-guessing game can be played with a group of children. Provide a small collection of instruments with very different timbres: perhaps a drum, a jingle bell, a maraca, a tambourine, and a xylophone block. You or the children can demonstrate the sound of each instrument. After each sound has been heard and children have learned the name of the instrument, hide all of the instruments behind a screen. From behind the screen, play one of the instruments, and encourage the children to either name the instrument or point to a photo of it. To make this more challenging, use similar instruments—perhaps all bells or all drums. To make it easier, use fewer instruments. After a few demonstrations, small groups of children can play this game without adult help.

Physical Development and Well-Being

OBSERVE AND LEARN:
Obstacle Courses for Large Motor Play

The teachers at Misty Meadow Early Learning Center collaborate on creating outdoor obstacle courses to challenge children's gross-motor skills and to give them new ways to practice their growing motor competence. The obstacle courses appear as a surprise once or twice a month, are different every time, and are met with the children's great enthusiasm. The teachers incorporate large boxes to crawl through, small boxes to jump over, a balance beam made of long wooden unit blocks, large plastic hoops to jump in and out of, a sturdy small table to crawl under or climb over, plastic traffic cones to weave through by walking or running or using a wheelchair, a limbo pole made from a broomstick held in place by two chairs, ring toss, chalk lines to jump over, and so on.

The obstacles provide exercise of such skills as moving from place to place, catching, throwing, bending, aiming, balancing, climbing, and jumping. The teachers plan with attention to the large motor needs and capabilities of individual children, provide a wide range of possibilities, and do not require (but may gently encourage) each child to try each station. Because the teachers work together on the obstacle courses, the effort of planning, setting up materials, and putting materials away is not overwhelming. The teachers have grown to enjoy the collegial challenge of coming up with new and interesting ways for children to have fun while practicing their full range of large motor competencies.

Perhaps one of the most obvious contributions of play is its contribution to children's physical development and well-being. Play provides a perfect context for children to develop their motor abilities. Imagine what it would be like if we could somehow prohibit children's physical play. Their opportunities for physical development would be restricted to purely functional activities and organized physical exercise. The play context provides serious motivation for physical activity and skill development. Playing with small snap-together blocks, lacing beads on a string, and accompanying a song with hand and finger movements are generally more meaningful activities than ten sets of finger exercises done solely for the purpose of exercise! Running in the context of rough-and-tumble play or playing a game of Duck-Duck-Goose is generally more engaging than following an instruction to run back and forth to the fence three times.

There is an interesting link between children's physical skills and their sense of overall competence. During the preschool years, as children develop their sense of competence and self-esteem, they tend to focus on aspects of their physical activity. As children progress into middle and later childhood, their focus turns more toward personality and psychological aspects of self. This is not surprising. The physical self and physical activities are directly observable. Consideration of the interior psychological self requires greater maturity and sophistication. Most teachers and parents can verify the frequency with which preschoolers draw their attention with shouts of, "Look what I can do!" and "Look at me!" Because physical behavior is important to children's growing sense of self, they will often choose to engage in physical play. This is one reason it is important to provide appropriate support and doable activities for children with disabilities that affect their motor skills.

Motor development is generally divided into categories of fine-motor, gross-motor, and perceptual-motor development. *Fine-motor development* involves using the hands and fingers to move small objects precisely and accurately. It includes such behaviors as picking up and placing objects; using scissors; and participating in fingerplays, drawing, and handwriting. *Gross-motor development* includes activities such as walking, running, jumping, skipping, and climbing; kicking, throwing, catching, and rolling; and bending, spinning, lifting, and stretching. *Perceptual-motor abilities* combine perception and motor action and include body awareness, spatial awareness, balance, and direction awareness. Some goals for motor development, based on recommendations in Marjorie Kostelnik et al.'s *Developmentally Appropriate Curriculum* and in the *Head Start Early Learning Outcomes Framework* are as follows:

- **Fine-motor/Perceptual motor**

  - Develops hand strength and dexterity

  - Manipulates writing, drawing, and art tools

- **Gross-motor/Perceptual motor**

  - Develops motor control and balance for a range of physical activities, such as walking, propelling a wheel chair or mobility device, skipping, running, climbing, and hopping

  - Develops motor coordination and skill in using objects for a range of physical activities such as pulling, throwing, catching, kicking, bouncing or hitting balls, and riding a tricycle

- **Physical health and well-being**

  - Gets sufficient rest and exercise to support healthy development

  - Possesses good overall health, including oral, visual, and auditory health, and is free from communicable and preventable diseases

Ideas for Supporting Fine-Motor Development through Play

Provide many opportunities throughout the day for children to play with materials that foster hand strength, dexterity, and eye-hand coordination. The list of possibilities is very long, and you can probably think of many more. Keep in mind that you may need to provide children with more or less direct guidance in skills such as how to wipe excess paint off of a paintbrush before using it; how to hold a string near the end to successfully string beads onto it; and how to soften clay before using it to mold, sculpt, or just squish. If you leave children to figure out all of these things on their own, they may become frustrated or bored and may abandon the activity. In addition to instruction, there are other ways to support children's ability to use fine-motor materials. For example, show a child how to hold scissors, keeping in mind that there are ways to make cutting more manageable by providing materials that are easier for children to hold and to cut. Cutting fringe on the edge of a sturdy piece of paper is usually easier than cutting out a drawn triangle or circle shape. A variety of types of scissors are available, some of which may be helpful to a child with fine-motor difficulty due to a disability. Many fine-motor activities can help children develop the abilities that will make it easier for them to learn to eventually form letters.

Some materials and activities to support fine-motor development:

- Lacing board
- Bead stringing
- Cutting
- Drawing utensils
- Pouring
- Small blocks
- Small snap-together blocks
- Nuts and bolts

- Clay or playdough
- Paintbrushes
- Glue applicators
- Puzzles
- Peg boards
- Tweezers
- Pompoms
- Droppers

Provide a segmented tray, such as one for making small ice cubes, tweezers, and small objects such as pompoms. Many children enjoy the challenge of picking up the objects with the tweezers and placing them in the small wells of the tray. Regular droppers can be difficult to use, but many school-supply merchants sell droppers that are inexpensive and easy for young children to control. Provide droppers, small containers of water, and something with many small suction cups, such as the back of a new bathtub mat or small suctioned soap dishes. Children can use the droppers to carefully place one or two drops in each little suction cup. To add further interest to the activity, you can provide several colors of water and a white suctioned surface. Children can make patterns or designs, or mix drops of different colors in the suction cups.

Ideas for Supporting Gross-Motor and Perceptual-Motor Development through Play

In addition to free access to the usual playground equipment, you can intentionally plan for gross-motor play on the playground. Teach and facilitate games and activities that involve a lot of large muscle and/or aerobic activity. Games can be noncompetitive or competitive or those in which a child competes only against her own previous performance. A few possibilities are listed below. If you don't know how to play these games (or if you have forgotten!), you can easily find directions with a quick web search.

- Tag
- Red Light, Green Light
- Head, Shoulders, Knees, and Toes
- Mother, May I?

- Relay Races
- Ring around the Rosy
- Hopscotch
- Monkey in the Middle

- Duck-Duck-Goose
- Ring Toss
- Bean Bag Toss
- London Bridge Is Falling Down

- Bowling
- Obstacle Courses
- Follow the Leader
- Hens and Chicks

Another important way to support children's large-motor development and aerobic activity is to allow for rough-and-tumble play. Research on rough-and-tumble play has grown in the past few decades. In addition to the physical benefits, the value of this form of play to children's emotional development and self-regulation is considerable. In the past, many teachers have attempted to ban this kind of play, often due to fear of fighting, escalation, agitation, and injury. Learning to distinguish rough-and-tumble play from actual aggressive behavior is an important first step. In *Big Body Play* by Frances Carlson, teachers are encouraged to pay attention to children's relaxed facial expressions, their willingness to participate, and their willingness to return to and extend the play. These are indicators that play—rather than actual fighting—is happening.

To support outdoor rough-and-tumble play, there should be at least 100 square feet of play space per child. This space should be free from fixed equipment and appropriate safety surfaces should be present.

■ ■

Concluding Thoughts

Play is a four-letter word, as are *grow, good, math, glad, read, draw, kids,* and *love.* Play is a crucial process in early learning. While there is more involved in high-quality preschool programming than play, play is an indispensable component of a high-quality program. Through play, young children learn and develop in the cognitive, language, physical-motor, emotional, social, and creative domains. They develop positive approaches to learning: curiosity, persistence, initiative, attentiveness, and cooperation. They gain important skills, concepts, and information in the areas of math, literacy, social studies, science, and the arts.

Play is a multifaceted phenomenon. There is a variety of types of play through which children may best learn and grow in different areas. Sometimes play is both initiated and directed by children, and there are many benefits to allowing children daily opportunities for this free play in which they make virtually all of the decisions. For example, children can develop initiative, make creative choices, and learn from mistakes and from the natural responses they receive from their physical and social environment. Free play offers the potential to meet a wide variety of learning goals.

In guided play, a teacher initiates and gently guides the child's play, with some particular goals in mind. The teacher does not co-opt or take over the child's play. The child maintains control of the ultimate direction in which the play goes, while the teacher's planning and guidance increase the potential for children to "bump into" important concepts and skills. This form of teaching through play maintains the qualities of motivation and high engagement that generally characterize play and help to make it such a natural medium for young children's learning.

In the current academic climate of often inappropriate use of testing and test data for purposes of accountability, the important place of play in the early childhood years is jeopardized. Inaccurate and incomplete understanding of the nature of play, as well as misinformation about how young children learn and develop in the preschool and primary years, seem to be leading to what many have labeled as a crisis in early education. To preserve play in preschool settings, preschool teachers can develop and use a variety of skills to support the quality of children's play and to support their learning of important learning dispositions, skills, and concepts through play.

References and Resources

Administration for Children and Families. 2015. *Head Start Early Learning Outcomes Framework: Ages Birth to Five.* Washington, DC: U.S. Department of Health and Human Services, Administration for Children and Families, Office of Head Start.

Ailwood, Jo. 2003. "Governing Early Childhood Education through Play." *Contemporary Issues in Early Childhood* 4(3): 286–299.

Almon, Joanne, and Edward Miller. 2011. "The Crisis in Early Education: A Research-Based Case for More Play and Less Pressure." Alliance for Childhood. www.allianceforchildhood.org

Barnett, Steven, et al. 2008. "Educational Effects of the *Tools of the Mind* Curriculum: A Randomized Trial." *Early Childhood Research Quarterly* 23(3): 299–313.

Barton, Erin. 2016. "Critical Issues and Promising Practices for Teaching Play to Young Children with Disabilities." In *Handbook of Early Childhood Special Education.* New York: Springer.

Bell, Janice, Jeffrey Wilson, and Gilbert Liu. 2008. "Neighborhood Greenness and 2-Year Changes in Body Mass Index of Children and Youth." *American Journal of Preventive Medicine* 35(6): 547–553.

Blasi, Maryjane, and Sally Hurwitz. 2002. "For Parents Particularly: To Be Successful—Let Them Play!" *Childhood Education* 79(2): 101–102.

Bodrova, Elena, Carrie Germeroth, and Deborah Leong. 2013. "Play and Self-Regulation: Lessons from Vygotsky." *American Journal of Play* 6(1): 111–123.

Bodrova, Elena, and Deborah Leong. 2006. *Tools of the Mind: The Vygotskian Approach to Early Childhood Education.* 2nd ed. Boston: Pearson.

Broadhead, Pat, Justine Howard, and Elizabeth Wood. 2010. *Play and Learning in the Early Years: From Research to Practice.* Los Angeles: Sage.

Brown, Stuart, and Christopher Vaughan. 2009. *Play: How It Shapes the Brain, Opens the Imagination, and Invigorates the Soul.* New York: Avery.

Carlson, Frances M. 2011. *Big Body Play: Why Boisterous, Vigorous, and Very Physical Play Is Essential to Children's Development and Learning.* Washington, DC: NAEYC.

Chalufour, Ingrid, and Karen Worth. 2004. *Building Structures with Young Children.* Washington, DC: NAEYC.

Charlesworth, Rosalind, and Karen Lind. 2007. *Math and Science for Young Children.* 5th ed. Boston, MA: Cengage.

Christie, James F., and Francis Wardle. 1992. "How Much Time Is Needed for Play?" *Young Children* 47(3): 28–32.

Church, Ellen Booth. 2015. *Getting to the Heart of Learning: Social-Emotional Skills across the Early Childhood Curriculum.* Lewisville, NC: Gryphon House.

Committee for Children. 2014. *The Second Step Early Learning Program.* Seattle, WA: Committee for Children.

Coplan, Robert, and Kimberly Arbeau. 2009. "Peer Interactions and Play in Early Childhood." In *Handbook of Peer Interactions, Relationships, and Groups.* New York: Guilford.

Copple, Carol, and Sue Bredekamp. 2009. *Developmentally Appropriate Practice in Early Childhood Programs Serving Children from Birth through Age Eight.* Washington, DC: NAEYC.

Cropley, Arthur. 2001. *Creativity in Education and Learning.* Abingdon, Oxon, UK: Routledge.

Daly, Lisa, and Miriam Beloglovsky. 2015. *Loose Parts: Inspiring Play in Young Children.* St. Paul, MN: Redleaf.

Diamond, Karen E., and Soo-Young Hong. 2010. "Young Children's Decisions to Include Peers with Physical Disabilities in Play." *Journal of Early Intervention* 32(3): 163–177.

Dickinson, David, and Joy Moreton. 1991. "Predicting Specific Kindergarten Literacy Skills from Three-Year-Olds' Preschool Experiences." Paper presented at the meeting of the Society for Research in Childhood Development, Seattle, WA.

Eggum-Wilkens, Natalie, et al. 2014. "Playing with Others: Head Start Children's Peer Play and Relations with Kindergarten School Competence." *Early Childhood Research Quarterly* 29(3): 345–356.

Elkind, David. 2007. *The Power of Play: Learning What Comes Naturally.* Boston, MA: Da Capo Press.

Fisher, Kelly, et al. 2013. "Taking Shape: Supporting Preschoolers' Acquisition of Geometric Knowledge through Guided Play." *Child Development* 84(6): 1872–1878.

Fjortoft, Ingunn. 2001. "The Natural Environment as a Playground for Children: The Impact of Outdoor Play Activities in Pre-Primary School Children." *Early Childhood Education Journal* 29(2): 111–117.

Fromberg, Doris P., and Doris Bergen. 2015. *Play from Birth to Twelve: Contexts, Perceptions, and Meaning.* New York: Routledge.

Frost, Joe, Sue Wortham, and Stuart Reifel. 2012. *Play and Child Development,* 4th ed. Boston, MA: Pearson.

Ginsburg, Herbert, and Kyoung-Hye Seo. 2009. "Mathematics in Children's Thinking." *Mathematical Thinking and Learning* 1(2): 113–129.

Ginsburg, Kenneth. 2007. "The Importance of Play in Promoting Healthy Child Development and Maintaining Strong Parent-Child Bonds." *Pediatrics* 119(1): 182–191.

Goksun, Tilbe, et al. 2013. "Forces and Motion: How Young Children Understand Causal Events." *Child Development* 84(4): 1285–1295.

Gronlund, Gaye. 2010. *Developmentally Appropriate Play: Guiding Children to a Higher Level.* St. Paul, MN: Redleaf.

Heidemann, Sandra, and Deborah Hewitt. 2010. *Play: The Pathway from Theory to Practice.* St. Paul, MN: Redleaf.

Henkes, Kevin. 1985. *Bailey Goes Camping.* New York: Mulberry.

Hirsh-Pasek, Kathy, and Roberta Golinkoff. 2003. *Einstein Never Used Flash Cards: How Our Children Really Learn—And Why They Need to Play More and Memorize Less.* Emmaus, PA: Rodale.

Hirsh-Pasek, Kathy, et al. 2009. *A Mandate for Playful Learning in Preschool: Presenting the Evidence.* New York: Oxford University Press.

Hughett, Kristy, Frank Kohler, and Donna Raschke. 2013. "The Effects of a Buddy Skills Package on Preschool Children's Social Interactions and Play." *Topics in Early Childhood Special Education* 32(4): 246–254.

Huizinga, Johan. 1949. *Homo Ludens: A Study of the Play-Element in Cultures.* London, UK: Routledge and Kegan Paul.

IBM Institute for Business Value. 2016. *Redefining Competition: Insights from the Global C-suite Study—The CEO Perspective.* Somers, NY: IBM Global Business Services.

Institute of Medicine and National Research Council. 2012. *From Neurons to Neighborhoods: An Update.* Workshop Summary. Washington, DC: The National Academies Press.

International Reading Association and NAEYC. 1998. *Learning to Read and Write: Developmentally Appropriate Practices for Young Children.* Joint Position Statement of the International Reading Association and NAEYC. *Young Children* 53(4): 30–46.

Jones, Elizabeth, and Gretchen Reynolds. 2011. *The Play's the Thing: Teachers' Roles in Children's Play*, 2nd ed. New York: Teachers College Press.

Jung, Eunjoo, and Bora Jin. 2014. "Future Professionals' Perceptions of Play in Early Childhood Classrooms." *Journal of Research in Childhood Education* 28(3): 358–376.

Kamii, Constance, and Rheta DeVries. 1993. *Physical Knowledge in Preschool Education: Implications of Piaget's Theory.* New York: Teachers College Press.

Katz, Esther, and Luigi Girolametto. 2013. "Peer-Mediated Intervention for Preschoolers with ASD Implemented in Early Childhood Education Settings." *Topics in Early Childhood Special Education* 33(3): 133–143.

Kemple, Kristen M. 2004. *Let's Be Friends: Peer Competence and Social Inclusion in Early Childhood Programs.* New York: Teachers College Press.

Kemple, Kristen M., Jacqueline Batey, and Lynn Hartle. 2004. "Musical Play: Creating Centers for Musical Play and Exploration." *Young Children* 59(4): 30–37.

Koralek, Derry. 2004. *Spotlight on Young Children and Play.* Washington, DC: NAEYC.

Kostelnik, Marjorie, et al. 2014. *Developmentally Appropriate Curriculum: Best Practices in Early Childhood Education,* 6th ed. Boston, MA: Pearson.

Levine, Susan, et al. 2011. "Early Puzzle Play: A Predictor of Preschoolers' Spatial Transformation Skill." *Developmental Psychology* 48(2): 530–542.

Lifter, Karen, Emanuel Mason, and Erin Barton. 2011. "Children's Play: Where We Have Been and Where We Could Go." *Journal of Early Intervention* 33(4): 281–297.

Lifter, Karen, et al. 2011. "Overview of Play: Its Uses and Importance in Early Intervention/ Early Childhood Special Education." *Infants and Young Children* 24(3): 225–245.

Lillard, Angeline, and Robert Kavanaugh. 2014. "The Contribution of Symbolic Skills to the Development of an Explicit Theory of Mind." *Child Development* 84(4): 1535–1551.

Lillard, Angeline, et al. 2013. "The Impact of Pretend Play on Children's Development: A Review of the Evidence." *Psychological Bulletin* 139(1): 1–34.

Lindsey, Eric, and Malinda Colwell. 2013. "Pretend and Physical Play: Links to Preschoolers' Affective Social Competence." *Merrill-Palmer Quarterly* 59(3): 330–360.

Logue, Mary Ellin, and Hattie Harvey. 2009. "Preschool Teachers' Views of Active Play." *Journal of Research in Childhood Education* 24(1): 32–49.

Lovasi, Gina, et al. 2008. "Children Living in Areas with More Street Trees Have Lower Prevalence of Asthma." *Journal of Epidemiology and Community Health* 62(7): 647–649.

Meacham, Sohyun, et al. 2014. "Preschool Teachers' Questioning in Sociodramatic Play." *Early Childhood Research Quarterly* 29(4): 562–573.

Meins, Elizabeth, et al. 2013. "Mind-Mindedness and Theory of Mind: Mediating Roles of Language and Perspectival Symbolic Play." *Child Development* 84(5): 1777–1790.

Mendoza, Jean, and Lilian Katz. 2008. "Introduction to the Special Section on Dramatic Play." *Early Childhood Research and Practice* 10(2). http://ecrp.uiuc.edu/v10n2/introduction.html

Misra, Madhusmita, et al. 2008. "Vitamin D Deficiency in Children and Its Management: Review of Current Knowledge and Recommendations." *Pediatrics* 122(2): 398–417.

Monighan-Nourot, Patricia, et al. 1987. *Looking at Children's Play: A Bridge between Theory and Practice.* New York: Teachers College Press.

NAEYC. 2009. *Developmentally Appropriate Practice: A Focus on Intentionality and Play.* DVD. Washington, DC: NAEYC.

NAEYC and NCTM. 2010. *Early Mathematics: Promoting Good Beginnings.* Joint position statement. Washington, DC: NAEYC.

National Council for the Social Studies. 2010. *National Curriculum Standards for Social Studies: A Framework for Teaching, Learning, and Assessment.* Washington, DC: National Council for the Social Studies.

NCTM. 2000. *Principles and Standards for School Mathematics.* Reston, VA: National Council of Teachers of Mathematics.

Nell, Marcia, and Walter Drew. 2013. *From Play to Practice: Connecting Teachers' Play to Children's Learning.* Washington, DC: NAEYC.

Nicolopoulou, Ageliki. 2010. "The Alarming Disappearance of Play from Early Childhood Education." *Human Development* 53(1): 1–4.

Parsons, Amy, and Nina Howe. 2013. "'This Is Spiderman's Mask.' 'No, It's Green Goblin's': Shared Meanings during Boys' Pretend Play with Superhero and Generic Toys." *Journal of Research in Childhood Education* 27(2): 190–207.

Piaget, Jean. 1962. *Play, Dreams, and Imitation in Childhood.* New York: W.W. Norton and Company.

Plucker, Jonathan, James Kaufman, and Ronald Beghetto. 2015. *What We Know about Creativity: Part of the 4C's Research Series.* Washington, DC: Partnership for 21st Century Learning. http://www.p21.org/storage/documents/docs/Research/P21_4Cs_Research_Brief_Series_-_Creativity.pdf

Ramani, Geetha. 2012. "Influence of a Playful, Child-Directed Context on Preschool Children's Peer Cooperation." *Merrill-Palmer Quarterly* 58(2): 159–190.

Ramani, Geetha, et al. 2014. "Preschool Children's Joint Block Building during a Guided Play Activity." *Journal of Applied Developmental Psychology* 35(4): 326–336.

Ranz-Smith, Deborah. 2007. "Teacher Perceptions of Play: In Leaving No Child Behind Are Teachers Leaving Childhood Behind?" *Early Education and Development* 18(2): 271–303.

Ranz-Smith, Deborah. 2012. "Explicating the Place of Play: Resolving Dilemmas of Research-to-Practice." *Journal of Early Childhood Teacher Education* 33(1): 85–101.

Raver, Cybele. 2002. "Emotions Matter: Making the Case for the Role of Young Children's Emotional Development for Early School Readiness." *Social Policy Report of the Society for Research in Child Development* 16(3): 1–20.

Reifel, Stuart, and Mac Brown. 2004. *Social Contexts of Early Education and Reconceptualizing Play (II).* Advances in Early Education and Day Care, volume 13. Bingley, UK: Emerald Group.

Rivkin, Mary S. 1995. *The Great Outdoors: Restoring Children's Right to Play Outside.* Washington, DC: NAEYC.

Rogers, Sue, ed. 2011. *Rethinking Play and Pedagogy in Early Childhood Education: Concepts, Contexts, and Cultures.* New York: Routledge.

Rose, Kathryn, et al. 2008. "Outdoor Activity Reduces the Prevalence of Myopia in Children." *Ophthalmology* 115(8): 1279–1285.

Rushton, Stephen. 2011. "Neuroscience, Early Childhood Education, and Play: We Are Doing It Right!" *Early Childhood Education Journal* 39(2): 89–94.

Rushton, Stephen, Anne Juola-Rushton, and Elizabeth Larkin. 2010. "Neuroscience, Play and Early Childhood Education: Connections, Implications, and Assessment." *Early Childhood Education Journal* 37(5): 351–361.

Russ, Sandra. 2014. *Pretend Play in Childhood: Foundation of Adult Creativity.* Washington, DC: American Psychological Association.

Sabol, Terri, and Robert Pianta. 2012. "Patterns of School Readiness Forecast Achievement and Socioemotional Development at the End of Elementary School." *Child Development* 83(1): 282–299.

Sandberg, Anette, and Ingrid Pramling Samuelsson. 2003. "Preschool Teachers' Play Experiences Then and Now." *Early Childhood Research and Practice* 5(1). http://ecrp.uiuc.edu/v5n1/sandberg.html

Saracho, Olivia, ed. 2012. *Contemporary Perspectives on Research in Creativity in Early Childhood Education.* Charlotte, NC: Information Age Publishing.

Shaw, D. G. 2005. "Brain Fitness for Learning." *New Teacher Advocate* 13(2): 6-7.

Sherwood, Sara, and Stuart Reifel. 2013. "Valuable and Unessential: The Paradox of Preservice Teachers' Beliefs about the Role of Play in Learning." *Journal of Research in Childhood Education* 27(3): 267–282.

Shonkoff, Jack P., and Deborah A. Phillips, eds. 2000. *From Neurons to Neighborhoods: The Science of Early Child Development.* Washington, DC: National Academies Press.

Singer, Dorothy, Roberta Golinkoff, and Kathy Hirsh-Pasek. 2006. *Play=Learning: How Play Motivates and Enhances Children's Cognitive and Social-Emotional Growth.* New York: Oxford University Press.

Sutherland, Shelbie, and Ori Friedman. 2012. "Preschoolers Acquire General Knowledge by Sharing in Pretense." *Child Development* 83(3): 1064–1071.

Sutherland, Shelbie, and Ori Friedman. 2013. "Just Pretending Can Be Really Learning: Children Use Pretend Play as a Source for Acquiring General Knowledge." *Developmental Psychology* 49(9): 1660–1668.

Tannock, Michelle. 2008. "Rough and Tumble Play: An Investigation of the Perceptions of Educators and Young Children." *Early Childhood Education Journal* 35(4): 357–361.

Taylor, Andrea, Frances Kuo, and William Sullivan. 2001. "Coping with ADD: The Surprising Connection to Green Play Settings." *Environment and Behavior* 33(1): 54–77.

Taylor, Andrea, and Frances Kuo. 2009. "Children with Attention Deficits Concentrate Better after a Walk in the Park." *Journal of Attention Disorders* 12(5): 402–409.

Trawick-Smith, Jeffrey, and Traci Dziurgot. 2011. "'Good-Fit' Teacher–Child Play Interactions and the Subsequent Autonomous Play of Preschool Children." *Early Childhood Research Quarterly* 26(1): 110–123.

Trawick-Smith, Jeffrey, Heather Russell, and Sudha Swaminathan. 2011. "Measuring the Effects of Toys on the Problem-Solving, Creative, and Social Behaviors of Preschool Children." *Early Child Development and Care* 181(7): 909–927.

Van Hoorn, Judith, et al. 2014. *Play at the Center of the Curriculum,* 6th ed. Boston, MA: Pearson.

Vygotsky, Lev. 1978. *Mind in Society: The Development of Higher Psychological Processes.* Cambridge, MA: Harvard University Press.

Webster-Stratton, Carolyn. 2011. *The Incredible Years: Parents, Teachers, and Children's Training Series.* Seattle, WA: The Incredible Years.

Weisberg, Deena, et al. 2015. "Making Play Work for Education: Research Demonstrates that Guided Play Can Help Preschool Children Prepare for Reading and Math Better than Free Play and Direct Instruction Alone." *Phi Delta Kappan* 96(8): 8–13.

Willis, Clarissa. 2015. *Teaching Young Children with Autism Spectrum Disorder.* Lewisville, NC: Gryphon House.

Youngquist, Joan, and Jann Pataray-Ching. 2004. "Revisiting 'Play': Analyzing and Articulating Acts of Inquiry." *Early Childhood Education Journal* 31(3): 171–178.

Zigler, Edward, Dorothy Singer, and Sandra Bishop-Josef, eds. 2004. *Children's Play: The Roots of Reading.* Washington, DC: Zero to Three.

Zins, Joseph, et al. 2004. "The Scientific Base Linking Social and Emotional Learning to School Success." In *Building Academic Success on Social and Emotional Learning: What Does the Research Say?* New York: Teachers College Press.

Index